The Berks & Hants Line

40 Years from the Lineside

Stephen Dance

Published by Platform 5 Publishing Ltd,
52 Broadfield Road, Sheffield, S8 0XJ. England.
Printed in the UK by Bell & Bain Ltd, Thornliebank, Glasgow, Scotland.
ISBN: 978 1 915984 17 3

Front cover upper: 50027 "Lion" brings 1A60, the 11.35 Newquay–Paddington round the curve at Hungerford Common on the afternoon of Saturday 19 July 1986. Hungerford station can be seen in the distance; this was the original terminus of the line until it was extended west to Devizes in 1862. It has been an unstaffed halt since 1971, when the original station buildings were demolished.

Front cover lower: On 20 June 2022, 59103 "Village of Mells" rounds Crofton Curve in Wiltshire with 6V18, the 11.20 Allington–Whatley empties. Not being the heaviest of trains, a Class 66 was usually assigned to this foray into Kent and back, so it was a pleasant surprise to find a Class 59 in charge on this occasion. This was a view that had been lost for many years behind a wall of trees and undergrowth, but following removal of the occupation overbridge that used to stand to the left of the photographer, clearance work had been undertaken, revealing this view of the curve.

Back cover: On a lovely spring 26 April 2022, 66413 "Lest We Forget" passes Adopters Lock on the Kennet and Avon Canal to the west of Crofton, with 6M20, the 10.38 Whatley–Churchyard Sidings. The canal features heavily in many photographs of the Berks and Hants as the railway closely follows it through some of the most attractive scenery along the route.

Previous page: 60019 "Port of Grimsby and Immingham" descends from Savernake at Brimslade Farm with 6B33, the Theale–Robeston empty tanks on 21 February 2015. This was a Saturday diversion away from the train's usual route via the Great Western Main Line due to engineering work. Usually hauled by a Class 60 this service is a popular target for photographers when running via the Berks and Hants line, as it represents one of the few opportunities in recent years to capture something other than a Class 59 or 66.

Above: During a visibly freezing morning on the Berks and Hants Line 66089 is in sole charge of 6Z53, the 05.13 Tytherington–Appleford, which is seen at Crofton Curve on 12 January 2022. The fields have a rime of frost and the road conditions that day could be described as a challenge. In addition to being slightly disappointed that the usual pair of locomotives did not appear, I found that the sun partially disappeared behind the only cloud in the sky moments before the train arrived, before coming back out two minutes later and then shining for the rest of the day!

Contents

Above: Taken from the abutments of the bridge that used to carry the Midland & South Western Junction Railway's line over the Berks & Hants route at Wolfhall, between Bedwyn and Pewsey, 50031 "Hood" approaches with 1C52, the 14.27 Paddington–Penzance on 3 August 1985. This is a typical 1980s summer Saturday scene on the Berks and Hants, when many additional passenger services were scheduled to accommodate the holidaymakers heading to and from the West Country.

Introduction

The Berks and Hants name, like the railway line it applies to, has always been something of an enigma as the scope of its meaning has changed over its near-180 year history. Its origins date back to the building of two lines by the Berks & Hants Railway (B&HR); Reading to Hungerford was completed in 1847 and Reading to Basingstoke, which swings away to the south from Southcote Junction, was completed in 1848. The purpose of these lines was an attempt, promoted by the Great Western Railway (GWR), to prevent the London & South Western Railway (L&SWR) from gaining access to Reading. By the time either line had opened, the B&HR had been absorbed into the GWR, having only existed as a separate company for little more than a year.

In 1859 the Berks & Hants Extension Railway company (B&HER) was formed to extend the line between Reading and Hungerford west to Devizes, where a connection was made with the GWR-built branch from Holt Junction on the Wilts, Somerset & Weymouth Railway's line through Trowbridge. The Berks & Hants Extension name was a complete misnomer, as only two miles of the line were in Berkshire, it went nowhere near Hampshire and most of it was in Wiltshire. The line to Devizes was built on a tight budget and opened in 1862. It closely followed the Kennet and Avon Canal for over ten miles, as the canal had been purchased by the GWR in 1851. It was built as a single track line, although the overbridges provided sufficient clearance for later doubling, and it had a large number of sharp curves, wooden culverts and underbridges, as little consideration had been given to it being anything other than a purely local transport link. The GWR then acquired the B&HER in 1882.

Both the original B&HR and B&HER lines were built to the GWR broad gauge. The section through Southcote Junction and on to Basingstoke was converted to mixed gauge in 1856, but the line west to Hungerford and Devizes remained broad gauge only until its conversion to standard gauge in 1874 (broad gauge trains to Basingstoke ceased running in 1869). Incredibly, the whole line from Southcote Junction to Devizes was re-gauged in only seven days.

In 1894 the GWR began upgrading the Berks and Hants, doubling the line, rebuilding the weak culverts and underbridges, and where possible easing the alignments. This was part of a larger plan to create a new shorter route from London to the West Country which involved joining several existing lines, such as the Berks and Hants, with newly built sections of railway. A new link from a junction just west of Patney on the original B&HER was built. This travelled west to Westbury, opening in 1900, and forms the Patney to Westbury section of today's main line. The new east to west line through to Cogload Junction near Taunton was completed in its entirety in 1906. Despite it being upgraded at a relatively early stage, the Berks and Hants remained a hostage to its more basic origins and even today it contains speed restrictions that are far below the capability of the trains that use it.

By the mid-1960s, with the exception of summer Saturdays, the Berks and Hants was under-utilised. With little local passenger or freight traffic, most of the stations west of Bedwyn had been closed by 1966 and the express passenger services from Paddington to Paignton, Plymouth and Penzance ran on a sparse two-hourly pattern, with many trains being combined and then split at Exeter. In addition, little had been done to modernise the route for many years, such that the line west of Southcote Junction in Reading was still mechanically signalled all the way to Westbury and beyond until as late as 1978. Together, these things meant that during the 1960s, serious consideration was given to at least partial closure of the Berks and Hants, with long-distance traffic being re-routed via Bristol. Fortunately that did not happen and passenger traffic took an upswing at the end of the 1960s when the Paignton, Plymouth and Penzance services were separated and their frequency increased. Then in 1970 the Foster Yeoman quarry at Merehead was connected to the freight line from Witham to Cranmore. This, together with trains from the nearby ARC-owned quarry at Whatley, led to an explosion of aggregate traffic on the Berks and Hants, fuelling the resurgence of the busy route it has now become.

So how do we define what the Berks and Hants represents today? Some use the name to describe the whole of the route from Reading to Cogload Junction in Somerset. Network Rail assigns

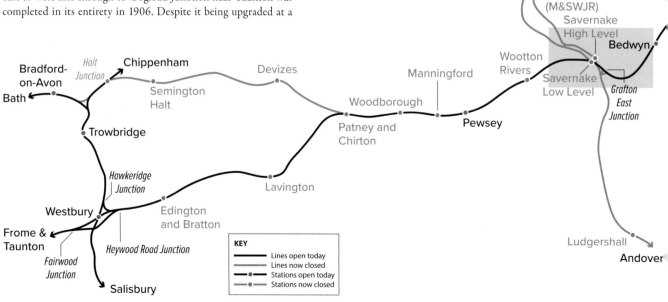

an Engineer's Line Reference (ELR) to every route in the country as part of its system to manage assets such as bridges, tunnels and level crossings. The Berks and Hants' ELR is BHL and this covers the line between Southcote Junction in the east, to just west of the former Patney and Chirton station, where the original, and now closed, B&HER diverged towards Devizes. While it is historically accurate, this definition results in the current end of the Berks and Hants being a featureless piece of double track where the ELR suddenly changes to SWY, for the Stert and Westbury Line. Operationally, today's logical definition is from Southcote Junction at Reading to Heywood Road Junction to the east of Westbury, but for the purposes of this book the area covered has been extended slightly to include Reading station and Fairwood Junction to the west of Westbury, so as to include the Westbury area.

I first visited the Berks and Hants Line in the summer of 1983 when a group of us made our way down to the West Country for a week of photographing Class 50s across Devon and Cornwall. From looking at maps and checking photographs in the books and magazines we possessed (there were of course no online resources back then), we concluded that we could reach most of the line's more photogenic locations by visiting Little Bedwyn, Crofton Curve and Fairwood Junction on a Saturday. A weekday visit wasn't deemed productive enough due to the lack of scheduled locomotive-hauled passenger services that ran on Mondays to Fridays. Little did I realise that 40 years later I would still be regularly visiting the line and discovering new locations and views along it!

A move for work in 1985 saw the Berks and Hants become a local line for me and many visits followed over the next few years. These were mainly on summer Saturdays, when the number of locomotive-hauled passenger services was much higher, providing capacity for the many holidaymakers that travelled to and from the West Country. It was only after I began making regular visits that I began to appreciate just how many potential photographic locations the line offered. Because of the twisty nature of the Berks and Hants, a suitable vantage point could almost always be found somewhere along the line, with the light in the desired position.

There was (and still is) much of interest on the Berks and Hants beyond its passenger services. The line was busy during the week carrying huge tonnages of aggregates from the Mendips. Unfortunately there was very little information to be found on when freight services ran back in the 1980s, and even when it started to become available in the 1990s, it was in printed form and the publications couldn't keep up with the many day to day schedule changes. It has only been since information has become more readily available through the internet, smartphones and websites that show what is running and where trains currently are, that it has been possible to reliably seek out freight trains. Back in the day you turned up at the lineside based on the interesting passenger services that were due and any freight that passed by was a bonus.

In 1984 Foster Yeoman, the operator of Merehead Quarry which moved large volumes of aggregates by rail, took the revolutionary step of privately purchasing a small batch of four new Class 59/0 locomotives from General Motors. These were delivered in 1986 and were joined by a fifth example in 1989. They were based on General Motors' highly successful SD40-2 model and proved to be far more reliable than anything that British Rail (BR) could offer. They were more powerful and their greater tractive effort meant they could handle significantly heavier loads. Amey Roadstone Construction (ARC) followed suit and their small batch of four Class 59/1s entered service in 1990. These more powerful engines led to a gradual reduction in the number of aggregate trains that ran, but an increase in the payloads. For example, one day in June 1989 I noted five eastbound loaded aggregate trains in a single hour (09.40–10.40). One was hauled by a Class 59, three by 56s and one by a pair of 37s. Today, I would probably only see one or two such trains within an hour, as the private freight companies strive to minimise the number of expensive timetable paths they use by running services formed of multiple portions that will then be split in London for onward delivery to separate destinations.

Traction on the Berks and Hants has become highly standardised over the years. In 1983, the vast majority of main line passenger

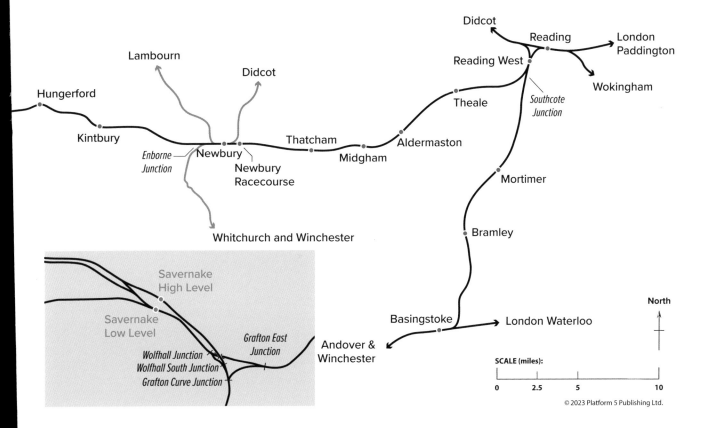

Above: On the morning of 13 September 2019, 59103 "Village of Mells" cautiously approaches Hungerford with 7A09, the extremely long 07.17 Merehead–Acton aggregate working, which can be seen snaking its way into the distance. This photograph epitomises freight traffic on the present-day Berks and Hants line, being formed of 43 wagons and grossing over 4000 tonnes.

services were High Speed Trains (HSTs), with Class 47s and 50s powering the remaining locomotive-hauled services. Today, all such long-distance passenger services are formed of Hitachi Intercity Express Train (IET) bi-mode units. Freight and other non-passenger workings in 1983 could see Classes 31, 37, 47, 50, and 56 being used and by 1989, that list had grown to include Classes 33 and 59, with Class 60s appearing in the 1990s. Today, the vast majority of freight services run behind Classes 59 or 66, offering less variety.

An ongoing theme referred to in the captions that follow is the never-ending encroachment of undergrowth and trees along the lineside. In the days of steam, not only was the lineside patrolled every day by staff who would remove saplings etc. as these began to grow, but the locomotives themselves did a good job of keeping growth down as they would often set fire to it. After diesels took over, the fire risk receded and the former system of lineside maintenance was abandoned, causing undergrowth to slowly take hold. Even so, by the 1980s the lineside was still reasonably open and uncluttered. It was only after privatisation and the formation of Network Rail's predecessor Railtrack in 1994, that lineside growth exploded. Railtrack was responsible for maintenance of the track and signalling infrastructure, but much of the maintenance work was sub-contracted to third party companies and seemingly anything outside the track cess was simply ignored. This has led to problems over the years since, as trees have matured close to the track, shedding their leaves each autumn, which in turn causes traction and braking issues for trains. It is so bad in some locations that passing trains can actually be hit by the branches of trees and undergrowth that have been allowed to grow close to the track, something that was almost unthinkable in the 1980s. Railtrack's successor, the

publicly owned Network Rail, now tends to target locations for undergrowth clearance if they become an operational problem, blitzing areas down to almost bare earth. Unfortunately the clearance works aren't usually followed up with any maintenance and so the growth tends to re-establish itself within a few years. This does create an ever-changing scene for the photographer though, as some photographic locations suddenly become available again after years, or even decades, while others slowly disappear behind a wall of greenery.

I will add a short note here about the cameras and equipment I have used over the years. The older 35mm negatives and transparencies were taken with either an Olympus OM-10 or a Canon AE-1, both with prime lenses from their respective manufacturers. The images have been scanned using a Nikon Coolscan V ED, with Photoshop and various other software packages being used to clean and sharpen the images. The digital shots have mainly been taken on Canon DSLRs, with 40D, 5D Mark III, and 5D Mark IV bodies all being used over the years, allied with Canon L Series zoom lenses of various sizes.

Finally, I would like to say a big thank you to the online communities of Flickr and Facebook, who have helped with the information in many of the captions. I am also grateful to Terry Gurd for allowing me to use some of his excellent medium format transparency scans to portray the ARC-liveried Class 59/1s which I mostly missed during a fallow period of photography. All the photographs are my own, except those that have been credited to Terry.

Stephen Dance
Autumn 2023

Chapter 1 – From Reading to Hungerford

Right: 47122 holds the enthusiasts' attention at Reading on 19 March 1983 as it brings a rake of bogie cement tanks through the station. I've not been able to identify the working, but as it's on the centre road it's likely to have come off the Berks and Hants Line. The tanks could be loaded, having begun from Westbury, or be empties returning from the unloading facilities at Theale. This busy scene is typical of Reading in the 1980s; a westbound High Speed Train (HST) has arrived at what then was Platform 4, while Southern Region 4-CIG electric multiple unit (EMU) 7405 has worked in from London Waterloo. The unit occupies one of the third rail electrified lines that were added when Reading Southern station closed in 1965 and Waterloo services were transferred to this station. Originally just one such platform was provided, until a second was added in 1975. On the right, Class 117 DMU set L424 is in the east end bay platform ready to form a local service to Maidenhead, Slough and London Paddington.

Below: On 13 April 1985, the lone enthusiast sitting in the traditional spot on the end of Reading's Platform 5 doesn't even bother to glance at 47050 as it brings a long rake of vans off the line from Reading West and Southcote Junction. The train is the daily Plymouth to Paddington empty newspaper working, and the leading two vehicles are newspaper sorting vans that were converted from Mark 1 full brake vehicles by sealing up some of the doors and removing the guards' compartments. The third vehicle is a Mark 1 passenger brake, which is probably there to provide seating and toilet facilities for the sorting staff.

Above: 56056 accelerates away from the main station building at Reading with a heavy load of aggregate during June 1982. The wagons are branded Tarmac, so this train will have been loaded in Frome North Yard and is now heading for Hothfield in Kent. There is still an occasional flow of such traffic to Hothfield, but this is now supplied from Whatley quarry as Frome North Yard has since become a housing estate. Although the main building is a handsome listed structure, the Reading station of the 1980s would never have won any prizes in a beauty contest. It did have some character though, despite BR's predilection at the time for painting anything that didn't move in grey. The scene here would change radically over the next 35 years. A limited redevelopment took place in 1989, which provided a new concourse and footbridge, but everything seen here except the listed main building was swept away during the major rebuild that took place between 2009 and 2015. In my view, this created a soulless concrete carbuncle, to which the addition of electrification infrastructure offered no visual improvement.

Right: On 13 January 2023, 66507 leads 59101 "Village of Whatley" at the head of 7C77, the 12.20 Wembley–Merehead empties at Ufton Nervet, which is to the west of Reading. 59005 "Kenneth J Painter" is also visible about half-way down the train. The Reading to Newbury section of the Berks and Hants line has been electrified since the end of 2018. The East Coast Main Line was electrified on a tight budget back in the late 1980s, with the overhead cables being largely supported on wire headspans or widely spaced masts. This proved to be fragile and the cause of numerous operational problems, so when the Great Western

Main Line electrification project began, much sturdier masts and overhead supports were used. As can be seen though, these are more visually intrusive and the uneven mast heights makes the scene look a bit of a mess. This photograph was taken from the approach embankment to the overbridge that replaced the level crossing at this location in 2016, following the tragic accident in 2004 in which seven people lost their lives when a westbound HST struck a car on the crossing and derailed.

Above: Class 165 Network Turbo unit 165116 is seen at Lower Padworth with a local service destined for Bedwyn on 14 February 2009. The signal on the right controls the exit from the Down Towney Loop which stretches to this point from just after the Ufton Nervet overbridge. The loop is in frequent use to regulate traffic on this double track line where train speeds can vary from 45 mph Class 7 freights to 100 mph+ Class 1 expresses formed of Hitachi IET units. The busy fuel, cement and aggregate terminals at Theale are just a couple of miles to the east. Westbound freight from Theale is often signalled out of the loops there and straight into Down Towney Loop to allow further movement to and from the terminals at Theale.

Above: 50015 "Valiant" approaches Frouds Lane overbridge between Aldermaston and Midgham with a westbound train on the evening of 26 August 1983. Normally it would be safe to assume this was a commuter service from Paddington to Newbury, Pewsey or Westbury, but this was the Friday of the August Bank Holiday weekend. There were a number of Friday only long-distance locomotive-hauled workings from Paddington to the West Country, especially during the summer months, and with it being the beginning of the Bank Holiday weekend, this could be an additional relief service.

Above: 50040 "Leviathan" rounds the curve through Midgham station with 1A50, the 10.00 Penzance–Paddington on 11 April 1987. The locomotive would receive the nameplates and crests from 50011 "Centurion" in July 1987 after the withdrawal of 50011 the preceding February. Midgham station is actually in the middle of Woolhampton, the village of Midgham being located about two miles further west. The old Great Western Railway (GWR) station sign, which has since been replaced by a standard Network Rail version, reads "Midgham For Douai School". This refers to the public school at the nearby Benedictine Douai Abbey which existed there from 1903 until its closure in 1999; the school was founded by the monastic order in 1615 and was originally located in France.

Above: 47573 "The London Standard" is seen just west of Midgham station hauling 1F22, the 12.40 Paddington–Newbury on 28 July 1989. The line here runs alongside the Kennet and Avon Canal and this photograph was taken from its towpath. Network SouthEast (NSE) livery had first appeared in 1986 and by 1989 it was displayed like this on the majority of services from Paddington to Oxford and Newbury. 47573 was a long time Stratford-allocated locomotive but had largely been based at Old Oak Common since March 1988, where it worked alongside the remaining Class 50s until they disappeared from NSE services out of Paddington in June 1990. 47573 then moved away from Old Oak Common in October 1990. All the locomotive-hauled NSE services from Paddington went over to DMU-operation during 1992, with services being worked by Class 165 and 166 Turbo units.

Above: Bone Mill Lane overbridge to the west of Newbury station lies just beyond the current end of the overhead catenary equipment. On 12 May 2022, 66035 "Resourceful" and 66194 have a load of aggregate in tow that is destined for the HS2 project. Unlike many such trains, this one did not originate from the Mendip quarries of Merehead or Whatley, but from Tytherington on the former Yate to Thornbury branch. The working is 6A53, the 05.13 Tytherington–Didcot which would usually terminate at Appleford, but on this occasion it stopped short of that destination for some reason. The southern part of the Didcot Newbury & Southampton Railway's line used to swing in from the left until its closure in 1964. This arrived at Enborne Junction, which was at a point towards the rear of the train. Sections of its trackbed to the south of Newbury were used during the upgrading of the A34 and the later building of the Newbury bypass which can be seen crossing the Berks and Hants Line in the background.

Above: On 2 December 2021, 59201 is seen west of Kintbury with 7A09, the 07.12 Merehead–Acton loaded aggregate working. 7A09 has been a feature of the Berks and Hants freight scene since the 1990s, when several separate workings were combined into one "Jumbo" train, reducing the number of expensive timetable paths that are used. The trains are split at Acton Yard, before the portions are worked forward to various terminals in the London area. Some of the separate sections are visible, with box wagons at the front and hoppers towards the rear. To the west of Newbury, the railway begins to closely follow the course of the Kennet and Avon Canal. From Hungerford westwards this is a legacy of its history, as the GWR had acquired the Kennet and Avon Canal in 1851, and already owned the B&HR and the line to Devizes, so building the Berks and Hants Extension Railway alongside the canal helped keep the costs down. Upon its opening, the GWR agreed to operate the B&HER for 21 years.

Above: Now that the internet provides advanced notice of train movements, not many out of the ordinary workings on the Berks and Hants Line escape the attention of enthusiasts. Consequently, there is usually a gallery of photographers waiting in locations where the view is clear of vegetation and the lighting is good. On 23 November 2022, 37688 "Great Rocks" passes some photographers to the east of Hungerford Common who are using different methods to gain extra elevation. The train is 5Z31, the 13.47 Reading Traincare Depot–Exeter Riverside barrier vehicle move. Having originated at Crewe and then picked up further vehicles at Reading, this train's final destination is Penzance, where it will arrive the following day to collect some redundant Mark 3 HST coaches which were to be scrapped at Newport.

Above: The driver of 60040 "The Territorial Army Centenary" gives a thumbs up to the photographer on the bridge as the locomotive winds through the reverse curves at Hungerford Common with 6B33, the 13.35 Theale–Robeston empty tanks on 23 February 2022. This is a long term traffic flow and whilst its routings have varied over the years, it has usually returned the empties to west Wales via the GWML. Between December 2019 and August 2022 however, it was routed via the Berks and Hants Line on weekdays. For some years this locomotive carried a one-off livery, in the form of a different shade of red, to celebrate the centenary of the Territorial Army. Note Hungerford Up Loop, which can be seen in the background. A loop used to exist on the Down side too, on the other side of the bridge towards Hungerford station, but the entrance to it was removed with the Reading Panel Western Extension resignalling scheme in 1978, although it survived as a refuge siding for a little longer.

Above: GWR finally dispensed with conventional full-length HST sets in 2019, ending nearly 43 years of service on the route out of Paddington. The final day of full-length HST operations for the GWR franchise was 1 June 2019, when a special commemorative train ran from Bristol to Paddington, then Paddington to Carmarthen (running via the Cotswold Line), returning to Paddington via a circuitous route and the day's lengthy itinerary ended with 1Z25, the 18.57 Paddington–Plymouth which is seen passing Hungerford Common. The train was named "The Flying Banana" after the somewhat derogatory nickname the HSTs acquired following their introduction in 1976. It was powered by the oldest and youngest power cars, 43002 "Sir Kenneth Grange" and 43198 "Driver Stan Martin/Brian Cooper". This was the last time a full-length HST with slam-door coaches ran on the Berks and Hants Line.

Right: Network Rail operates regular test trains to check and measure its infrastructure. In recent times, the freight operator Colas has usually provided the traction for these. On 20 May 2020, 37612 passes Hungerford Common at the head of 1Z22, the 08.20 Tyseley–Bristol High Level Siding, with 37610 on the rear. 1Z22 was scheduled to run via Worcester, the Cotswold Line, Oxford and Didcot, then head west along the GWML, before turning south at Thingley Junction for a visit to

Weymouth. However, due to an incident with two IETs hitting a cow on the line at Wootton Bassett things didn't go to plan that day. Some other photographers and I were waiting for the 37s on the GWML near Shrivenham when it was noticed on the online signalling diagrams that the road had been set for 1Z22 to travel from Didcot to Reading rather than via Swindon. Then followed an immediate exodus of enthusiasts who made the drive over the Downs to Hungerford to chase the diverted train. I arrived with just enough time to park the car and run up onto the bridge before capturing this view!

Above: Class 70s are not the most frequent of visitors to the Berks and Hants Line, but do appear from time to time, mainly as seen here, in the form of Colas-owned examples on infrastructure workings. On 29 September 2023, 70809 passes Hungerford Common hauling 6M40, the 11.42 Westbury–Cliffe Hill Stud Farm ballast empties which had been diverted from its usual route via Melksham and Swindon at short notice due to emergency track repairs taking place at Trowbridge.

Above: 47066 is seen at the head of the daily empty newspaper van train from Plymouth, 3A27 to London Paddington, on a fine late summer's morning of 7 September 1985. At the time, this working was my usual planned opening shot for summer Saturday visits to the Berks and Hants, as it was a reliable timekeeper. The traction could vary, but it was mostly hauled by Class 31s or 47s in 1985 and Class 50s became more common in 1986. The course of the now-lifted Down Goods loop can be seen to the left of the newspaper vans.

Right: The view from the north side of the line at Hungerford Common is only available with the sun over the shoulder very early in the morning during high summer. Taken at 06.16 on the blisteringly hot day of 21 July 2021, while it was still comfortable to be outside, 66149 catches the rising sun while working 6M32, the 02.52 Tytherington–Calvert. Calvert is on the former Great Central line, to the north of Aylesbury, and was being used at the time as a delivery

terminal for the aggregates required for the HS2 project. That function ceased around the end of September 2021, as construction work necessitated closure of the site and the track south to Quainton Road was lifted. These deliveries have since recommenced and now run via Aylesbury to a new terminal that is located to the south of Quainton Road.

Above: On the warm springlike afternoon of 22 March 2022, 60017 passes Hungerford Common with 6B33, the 13.35 Theale–Robeston empty tanks. The Class 60s were the last diesel locomotive class that BR introduced before privatisation, but by 2009 their use was at a low ebb. Coming up to 20 years old, many were in need of major overhauls and failures were common. Having inherited a large fleet of Class 66s after its takeover of EWS, DB Schenker did not want to invest in maintaining the Class 60s if it could use its newer Class 66s. In addition, the company had plenty of spare locomotives due to the economic downturn following the 2007/8 financial crisis. This led to many Class 60s being stored in the open at Toton depot near Nottingham and of the 100 built, only about ten would be active at any one time, in order to cover the most demanding duties, which included these Robeston to Theale services. However, the prodigious haulage capabilities and fuel efficiency of the 60s earned them a reprieve, as will be explained in later captions.

Chapter 2 – Hungerford to Crofton

Above: On 12 May 2022, 66035 "Resourceful" and 66194 descend towards Hungerford double heading 6A53, the 05.13 Tytherington–Didcot at Standers Foot Crossing. This train was scheduled to wait for about an hour in Hungerford Up Loop so the opportunity was taken to obtain another shot of it at Bone Mill Lane, Newbury, as seen on page 11. It is descending on a very gentle gradient of 1 in 1775 on the descent from Savernake Summit. The more serious climbing is for westbound trains, with the ascent beginning at Great Bedwyn, although in recent times this hasn't been much of a challenge for the modern traction, as little in the way of heavily loaded services are routed that way.

Above right: 59101 "Village of Whatley" takes 6A09, the 07.12 Merehead–Acton towards Hungerford on the cold winter's morning of 8 December 2022. It was running as a Class 6 train on this occasion, with a maximum speed of 60 mph, as the train was only formed of 24 wagons and the consist included no 45 mph-restricted vehicles. Single 59s are now few and far between on this working, which only runs as such when a second locomotive is not required to take one of the portions forward from Acton. When this photograph was taken, the sun was beginning to melt the frost, although temperatures in the shadows were still well below zero.

Right: 50050 "Fearless" is seen approaching Oak Hill overbridge near Froxfield in charge of 1A69, the 14.48 Paignton–Paddington on 3 August 1985. The view here is now unrecognisable, with mature trees and large bushes either side of the track, and a conifer plantation now stands on the first ridge in the background, blocking out the far wooded hillside. In addition, this angle from the north side of the bridge is no longer possible due to vegetation growth. A serious accident was narrowly avoided here on 22 February 2015, when a large lorry tried to use the very narrow road to Little Bedwyn. The driver found he could not traverse the adjacent canal bridge and while attempting to reverse back around the S bend to the A4, the rear of the lorry struck and demolished the eastern parapet of the bridge that crosses the railway here. Consequently, 13 tonnes of debris was deposited onto the track and this was then struck at high speed by the HST forming the 16.34 Paddington–Penzance. The front of the train was lifted by the impact, but fortunately it did not derail, and after an emergency brake application it came to a stand 800 yards further on. Luckily no one was injured.

Above: In striking mustard yellow and grey ARC livery, 59102 "Village of Chantry" passes Froxfield Bottom Lock No. 70 whilst in charge of 7A09, the 06.35 Merehead–Acton on 12 April 1995. Delivered in 1990, the four Class 59/1s were initially used on ARC's services to and from Whatley Quarry, but in 1993 ARC, together with Foster Yeoman, founded Mendip Rail and pooled their resources to better manage fleet availability. From then, the sight of ARC livery locomotives hauling Foster Yeoman wagons and vice-versa became common. *Terry Gurd*

Above: Almost exactly 26 years later, on 13 April 2021, another visit to Froxfield Bottom Lock No. 70 found 59101 "Village of Whatley" casting a reflection into the Kennet and Avon Canal while working 7A74, the 08.32 Whatley–Theale. Perfect reflections here are virtually never possible as water is entering the lower level of the canal from a spillway on the left near the lock gates. As can be seen by comparison with the previous picture, this location has seen significant changes due to tree growth and is now far less open than it once was. Another change is that the ex-ARC locomotives now wear the livery of Hanson.

Above: Just west of Fairfield Foot Crossing, 66013 takes a rake of empty Yeoman JHA hopper wagons westward with 7C74, the 15.35 Theale–Merehead on 7 September 2016. When Mendip Rail was formed in 1993, the company contracted operation of its train services to British Rail. After privatisation that passed to EWS and then onto DB Schenker when it subsequently acquired EWS. By the time this photograph was taken in 2016, DB Schenker had been rebranded as DB Cargo, which meant that this livery had become very out of date. At the time, the Class 59/0s and 59/1s were still owned by Mendip Rail, but the 59/2s were owned by DB Cargo as the company had inherited these after EWS purchased them in 1998. Class 66s were also used on the quarry trains, but generally only on lighter services as their 75 mph gearing limited the load they could work solo over Savernake Summit.

Above: 60028 and its matching rake of box wagons look smart in bright blue Cappagh livery on 23 March 2022. The Class 60 is operated by DC Rail, which was acquired by the Cappagh group of companies in 2017. It passes the picturesque scene at Little Bedwyn, with the church, railway and Kennet and Avon Canal all next to each other. The working is 6Z50, the 09.01 Willesden–Machen Quarry empties, a short term, irregular aggregate flow associated with the HS2 project. With the vast majority of aggregate wagons on the Berks and Hants now smothered in graffiti, it was refreshing to see this locomotive and rake of wagons remaining clean and tag free throughout 2021 and 2022. Sir Felix Pole, General Manager of the GWR from 1921 to 1929, was born in the village here in 1877, and the churchyard is his final resting place following his death in 1956.

Above: 47623 "Vulcan" passes the postcard-like scene at Little Bedwyn, complete with the local art class, the participants of which can be seen painting views of the canal, village and church. The train is 1C46, the 13.36 Paddington–Plymouth and the date is 22 June 1989. This has always been one of the signature locations on the Berks and Hants Line, especially back in the 1970s when Class 52 "Western" diesel-hydraulics sped past the then-abandoned canal and its derelict lock gates. This more modern vista was available for a time after the row of saplings between the canal and railway were removed in the late 1980s, and before the beech hedge grew too high in the mid-1990s. Today, the entire village and the railway line are hidden behind a wall of vegetation.

Above right: 47405 "Northumbria" makes a surprise appearance on 1A33, the 08.50 Paignton–Paddington, which is seen passing the lock at Little Bedwyn on 28 September 1985. The first 20 Class 47s to be built had a variety of technical differences to the rest of the fleet, one of which was an additional generator for the train heating. That led to 47401–47420 being nicknamed Generators and as they were Eastern Region machines, they were not common on the Berks and Hants Line. 47405 was allocated to Gateshead during the 1980s and when this photograph was taken it had just six months left in service. It became only the sixth Class 47 to be withdrawn in March 1986, and the first for a reason other than being "damaged beyond economic repair". Although the beech hedge that ruins the view from the bridge today had yet to be planted, the classic open vista wasn't available during much of the 1980s due to the row of saplings that can be seen between the canal and railway.

Right: Power car 43041 "Meningitis Trust Support for Life" leads the First Great Western HST set that forms 1A76, the 05.05 Penzance–Paddington past Little Bedwyn on a sunny 4 September 2013. 43041 remained in service until it was retired in 2022 and was then scrapped during the summer of 2023. The saplings seen in the previous photograph have been removed, but a beech hedge now separates the railway from the canal lock and 28 years of tree growth have significantly changed the view.

Left: Class 33s have never been particularly common on the Berks and Hants Line, but became regular visitors for a while, when they worked in pairs from the late 1980s, moving ballast from Meldon Quarry for use by the Network SouthEast sector. Here we see 33118 and 33002 returning west with 6V96, the 09.50 Tonbridge–Meldon Quarry ballast empties on 22 June 1989. Note the two-character Southern Region headcode on the leading locomotive, the displays of which have been wound round by the crew to display 96, which are the last two digits of the train's headcode. From the 1980s it became cheaper to source similar quality stone from Scotland and transport this by sea. Consequently, Meldon Quarry was mothballed in 2011, with the possibility that it could be re-opened if necessary. To date the quarry has not been re-opened and it is now designated a geological Site of Special Scientific Interest.

Below left: The afternoon of 23 August 2014 saw heavy showers developing as clumps of dark clouds drifted past Church Foot Crossing, Great Bedwyn. Fortunately these were a mile or two to the north east, with the bonus of blue sky behind me. Combining the cloudscape with sunshine and the bright red corporate livery of DB Schenker's 59203 resulted in this attractive photograph of 6V51, the 14.35 Churchyard Sidings–Westbury empties.

Above: The Venice Simplon Orient-Express Pullman stock has been seen on the Berks and Hants route for many years. Currently marketed as the British Pullman by Belmond, the traction when this is diesel hauled is usually one of DB Cargo's Pullman-liveried Class 67s. 67024 is seen passing Great Bedwyn on 29 September 2021, starting the challenging climb towards Savernake Summit. It is ascending at 1 in 300 and this will soon steepen to 1 in 175, then to 1 in 145, culminating with a 1 in 106 section. This was an empty coaching stock move, running as 5Z81, the 12.20 Newbury Racecourse–Salisbury East; the train's passengers were visiting the races at Newbury and would be transferred to Salisbury by road, where they would pick up the train home. The church in the background is St Mary's at Great Bedwyn. It was built in the 12th century, but a place of worship has stood here for over a thousand years, as the remains of an earlier Saxon church that dates back to the 10th century lies beneath the current Norman building. The church contains a memorial to Sir John Seymour, father of King Henry VIII's wife Jane Seymour, and grandfather of King Edward VI.

Above: 59103 "Village of Mells" approaches Beech Drive Crossing, as it works hard with the lengthy train of empties that forms 7C64, the 15.24 Acton–Merehead on 8 September 2016. Considering the gradient is 1 in 175 at this point, it is surprising that Network Rail has not undertaken any lineside maintenance here; the proximity of the large number of trees so close to the track is likely to prove troublesome for adhesion during autumn.

Above: The lengthening shadows are reaching across the field beside the line at Beech Drive Crossing as IET 800032 heads west towards Crofton with 1C90, the 17.04 Paddington–Penzance on 10 August 2021. The Class 800 bi-mode units here are obviously working on diesel power and have engines that can produce a maximum power of 940 hp when starting. The almost identical Class 802s were specified with a higher rated engine output range and a different power curve that assists them when working over the demanding gradients and sharp curves of South Devon and Cornwall. They also have a larger brake resistor that helps reduce brake pad wear. In practice however, Class 800s also work services through to Penzance.

Above: 50005 "Collingwood" brings 1A33, the 08.50 Paignton–Paddington past the Kennet and Avon Canal's Crofton Lock No. 62 on the beautiful summer Saturday of 15 June 1985. The Berks and Hants Line was full of interest on Saturdays between May and the end of September during the mid-1980s, with plenty of locomotive-hauled passenger services catering for the holidaymakers travelling to and from the resorts of Devon and Cornwall.

Above: Photographed on the same day, Saturday 15 June 1985, 50050 "Fearless" heads 1C25, the 09.40 Paddington–Penzance past canal bridge No. 99, from which the previous picture was taken. Also known as "The Bridge to Nowhere", it crosses the canal but only as far as the railway boundary. It was designed by the canal engineer John Rennie and is thought to be his first skew arch, with the courses of bricks in the arch laid at an angle. It was originally intended to form part of a scenic ride for the Earl of Aylesbury, the owner of Tottenham House. This was to run through the property's grounds, through which the Kennet and Avon Canal flows, and align with the Grand Avenue in Savernake Forest, but the two rides were never joined up. The bridge was in a bad state of repair for many years and had concrete tank traps installed on it during the early part of World War II. This was done as part of GHQ Stop Line Blue, which was part of the final line of defence in the event of a German invasion.

Below: Bringing back memories of the diesel-hydraulic era on the Berks and Hants Line, D1015 "Western Champion" runs alongside the Kennet and Avon Canal at Bridge No. 99 hauling The Royal Duchy railtour from Paddington to Penzance on 5 April 2008. On this date the loco was masquerading as D1068 "Western Reliance".

Bottom: A mile to the north-east of where 165110 is seen and these units would be an everyday sight, but appearances west of Great Bedwyn are rare as they are not scheduled to work west of Bedwyn station. The date is 30 March 2013, when work on rebuilding Reading station had closed all access to the Berks and Hants Line except for the western bay platforms on the south side. As a result, 165s were operating a shuttle service between Reading and Westbury. The work coincided with the 65th annual canoe race from Devizes to Westminster and two competitors can been seen paddling towards Crofton Bottom Lock No 63.

Bottom: Class 50s used to race past this point every day in the mid-1980s, but by the 2020s it had been over 30 years since I had last witnessed one passing here. 50007 "Hercules" takes the Belmond British Pullman stock past Bridge No. 99 on 18 June 2022, with 1Z50, the 08.00 London Victoria–Exeter St Davids Devon Pullman railtour. The return working was via the former London & South Western Railway route through Salisbury.

Above: This First Great Western (FGW) HST set is in FGW Barbie Pink Swoop livery, with power car 43189 "Railway Heritage Trust" leading. It is framed by canal bridge No. 99, as the train heads west on 7 July 2007. Apart from a few experiments in the 1980s and early 1990s, and a batch that received Paxman 12VP185L units in the late 1990s, most HST power cars retained their original Paxman Valenta engines until 2005 when FGW began replacing these with MTU 16V4000 engines. The scheme was completed at the end of 2007.

Above: 59001 "Yeoman Endeavour" approaches Crofton with 6C31, the 10.08 Theale–Whatley empties on 29 September 2021. The locomotive wears Aggregate Industries livery, as Foster Yeoman was acquired by the Holcim Group in 2006 and is now part of its Aggregate Industries subsidiary. Note the commemorative, but not functional, bell that was fitted by General Motors on one cab end.

Chapter 3 – Crofton to Savernake

Above: 66616 brings a lengthy rake of empty hopper wagons of various types past Crofton Crossing on a sparkling winter's day, 12 January 2022. The train is 6C31, the 10.08 Theale–Whatley. After Freightliner took over the Mendip Rail contract in November 2019, Class 66/6s began to appear on these workings. The sub-class was introduced in 2000 with lower ratio gearing, giving them a top speed of 65 mph, as opposed to 75 mph for the standard Class 66s. This allows them to handle the same loads as a Class 59 over the Berks and Hants route.

Below: 50001 "Dreadnought" is reflected in the waters of the Kennet and Avon Canal at Crofton on 7 September 1985, as it climbs the 1 in 183 gradient towards the canal pumping station and Crofton Curve with 1C29, the 10.18 Paddington–Paignton. The black diamond shape, which is visible above the left side of canal bridge No 100 in the background, is the vintage weight restriction sign that is still in place today. Nowadays, this section of canal has boats moored along it on an almost permanent basis, but back in the mid-1980s visiting craft were much rarer, as the canal was a dead end at Crofton and obstructions remained further east towards Reading. Restoration of the final section just beyond the canal pumping station was not completed until 1990.

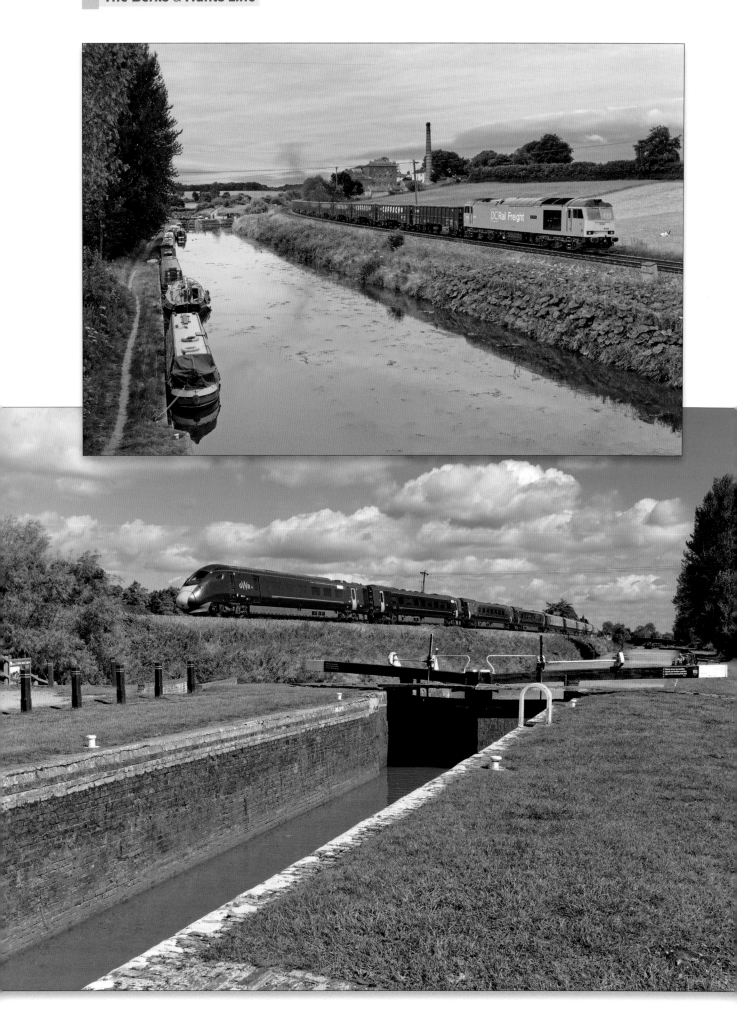

Above left: As well as the intermittent aggregate workings from Machen Quarry near Newport in 2021 and 2022, DC Rail also had a similar flow that originated from the old freightliner terminal in Bristol. This usually saw empties being taken west down the Berks and Hants early in the morning, before the loaded wagons returned during the late afternoon or early evening. Annoyingly, both would be against the natural lighting should the sun be out. On this rare occasion though, due to staff shortages, the loaded working was held at Bristol and the empties travelled back the next morning. 60029 "Ben Nevis" recovers from a signal check by Crofton Pumping Station with 6Z34, the 06.00 Bristol FLT–Willesden on 6 July 2022.

Left: Hitachi-built IET set 800314 swings right into the start of Crofton Curve past Crofton Lock No. 60 with 1C77, the 10.33 Paddington–Paignton on 4 September 2019. The GWR livery of dull, almost British Racing Green has not been hailed as a universal success, especially by photographers. It needs to be illuminated by full sun to really see the colour properly, and against a green background or in dull conditions, the train can disappear into the scenery.

Above: This is a scene that hasn't changed much in over 50 years, despite tree growth. 59206 "John F Yeoman Rail Pioneer" passes Crofton Canal Pumping Station as it drops down Savernake Bank and heads towards Bedwyn with 7A17, the 10.28 Merehead–Colnbrook on 4 September 2019. The lake in the foreground is Wilton Water; this was created to store and supply water to the canal, and keep it topped up. The pumping station dates back to 1809 and has been owned by the Kennet and Avon Canal Trust since 1968. The Trust has restored the pumping station, which contains the world's oldest working beam engine; this was installed in 1812, is still in its original building and it remains capable of pumping water.

Above: On 3 August 1985 50050 "Fearless" brings a westbound summer Saturday working round Crofton Curve and past the pumping station. Based on the adjacent negatives from the scanned strip, this is believed to be 1C29, the 10.18 Paddington–Paignton. The top 36-foot section of the pumping station chimney was removed in the 1950s as it was in a poor condition. It then transpired that the shortened chimney was unable to provide sufficient draught for the boilers to function properly and so the steam engines were abandoned and electric pumps were installed, even though by the late 1950s parts of the canal were so rundown they were only navigable by canoe. When the Kennet and Avon Canal Trust steamed the engines again in the 1970s, an electric fan was installed to improve the draught. Work to restore the chimney to its full height of 82 feet then took place in 1996 and 1997. Water is now pumped by steam on several days each year as a demonstration. In 2009 the modern electric pumps failed, and after British Waterways contacted the trust, the pumping station operated on steam power for a period until repairs could be made.

Above: Now more than four decades old, this is one of my earliest Berks and Hants photographs. On 27 August 1983, 31120 was at the head of 3A27, the Plymouth–Paddington empty newspaper vans. The eastbound train is seen on Crofton Curve, where the line swings through nearly 90 degrees in less than half a mile. This is the sharpest curve on the whole line; until the 1950s the speed limit here was 50 mph and even today, the sharpness of the curve necessitates a 70 mph restriction. The road bridge over the canal can be seen to the left of the rear coaches, but when this photograph was taken the canal itself was just a weed filled ditch that was awaiting restoration. The weight restricted occupation bridge that is visible above the locomotive was still in regular use at the time by the local farmer, but was removed in 2016 as by then it hadn't seen any motorised traffic in many years.

Right: Less than 30 minutes after sunrise, which revealed the frost-coated fields behind the train, on 12 January 2022, 59101 "Village of Whatley" rounds Crofton Curve at the head of 7C29, the 06.40 Acton–Merehead empties. The first wagon in the consist is an HOA hopper that was built for Mendip Rail by Touax Rail in Poland and was delivered in 2020. After nearly two years in service it has somehow managed to steer clear of the graffiti "artists".

Below: Looking in the other direction, on 7 September 1985 50010 "Monarch" brings a mixed rake of Mark 2 stock westward round Crofton Curve at the head of 1C52, the 14.27 Paddington–Penzance. Of note in this photograph is the lack of parked cars at the roadside. In more recent times the road here can resemble a car park during the summer weekends! Since the canal was fully restored, it has become a popular spot for boat owners to access and resupply their craft, whereas it was much quieter in the mid-1980s.

Above: Hastings Class 201 diesel-electric multiple unit 1001 rounds Crofton Curve on 19 June 2010, forming 1Z82, the 06.31 Hastings–Minehead "West Somerset Limited" railtour. The trailing motor coach is named "Mountfield". The middle two vehicles are Mark 1 stock from 4-CEP and 4-BIG EMUs, and the difference in body profile is immediately obvious, with the Hastings units having been built to a narrower design, in order to fit the restricted loading gauge of the tunnels on the Charing Cross to Hastings line.

Above right: Colas Rail operated a fleet of ten Class 60s from 2014 through to 2018 when it sold them to GBRf. During that time, these striking yellow, orange and black Tugs were not often seen on the Berks and Hants Line to the east of Westbury, unless they were diverted over the route. One such working that could be subject to weekend diversions was 6V62, the 11.12 Tilbury Riverside–Llanwern steel empties. This ran regularly on Saturdays for a number of years and would normally be routed via the Great Western Main Line. 60076 did the honours on 18 April 2015 and is seen at Crofton Curve.

Right: On 10 October 2022, 59202, which had only been named "Pride of Ferrybridge" a few weeks earlier, rounds Crofton Curve with 6Z60, the 11.02 Neasden–Merehead empties. This shot was taken from the embankment that used to lead up to the farm occupation bridge that is visible in the photograph of 31120 on page 32. For many years this view was not possible as it was completely blocked by trees and undergrowth. The permanent way staff of the steam era would not be happy with the trees and bushes that are now allowed to grow at the lineside, as illustrated by the vegetation to the left of the locomotive.

Above: 60020 "The Willows" is seen from a high angle on Crofton Curve with 6B33, the 13.35 Theale–Robeston empty tanks on 13 April 2021. As the weight of the normal consist for the inbound loaded tanks is more than a single 75mph-geared Class 66 can handle over the 1 in 93 Stormy Bank in Wales, in 2010/11 DB Schenker trialled pairs of 66s and single 59/2s on the service, with a view to these replacing the remaining Class 60s that required expensive overhauls. Neither were totally successful and couldn't come near the Class 60s' fuel efficiency, so in 2011 the Super 60 programme was announced to overhaul and improve an initial batch of seven of the class. At the time of writing in 2023, DB Cargo (formerly DB Schenker) still operate around 21 Class 60s and a further 14 have been overhauled and sold, and are now in service with other freight operators. It is now a decade since many of the DB Cargo Class 60s received their last heavy maintenance and they are again approaching the point where major expenditure will be required, leaving the future of these 30-year-old locomotives looking uncertain.

Above right: 37676 "Loch Rannoch" and 37685 "Loch Arkaig" ease into the start of Crofton Curve at the former Grafton East Junction with 1Z27, the 10.30 Exeter St Davids–Preston on 6 November 2011. This railtour was a one-way move in order to return the stock from the previous day's Jorvik Explorer III tour (from Exeter to York and return) back north. This train had no official name but was referred to as the Sunday Positioning Growler. The junction here was where Grafton Curve met the Berks & Hants Line, arriving from the south, as seen on the left. The curve was built by the GWR in 1905 to provide a south to east connection with the Midland & South Western Junction Railway's (M&SWJR) line from Andover and Ludgershall. It completed a railway triangle, as the M&SWJR route had previously only had a south to west curve, joining the Berks and Hants at Wolfhall Junction to the west. Grafton East signal box used to stand in the area on the left; the box was usually left switched out of use and was only manned when needed. Grafton Curve never saw any scheduled passenger services, as its primary purpose was to carry military traffic. Outside of wartime, only occasional troop trains, excursions and enthusiast specials would traverse it, and on busy Newbury race days, locomotives would be turned on the triangle here to avoid congestion on Newbury shed and its turntable. The curve was closed in 1957 and the track was subsequently lifted.

Right: In recent years, the locomotive off the inbound loaded tanks from Robeston to Theale has been scheduled to run light engine from Theale to Didcot and back for fuel, before it works the empties back to West Wales. Occasionally, the opportunity is taken to substitute a Class 66 at Didcot if a fault is found on the original locomotive. I believe this is what had happened on 29 September 2021, when 66130 turned up between Crofton and Wolfhall with 6B33, the 13.35 Theale–Robeston empty tanks. The gradients are slightly easier in the westbound direction, both on the Berks and Hants Line and in Wales, plus the weight of empty tanks is more manageable, so a single Class 66 has no problem with the load.

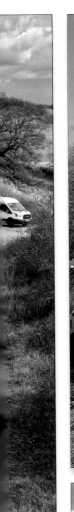

Above: 59203 is seen at the head of a very short 7A09, the 07.12 Merehead–Acton on 6 October 2022. The train is between Wolfhall and Crofton, with Crofton Lock No. 56 visible on the left. The latter part of 2022 was a period of unrest on the railways, and this particular week saw strike action taken by three different unions. As a result, the passenger operator GWR was running no trains over the Berks and Hants that day, but freight was unaffected. That meant that on this occasion there was no need for freight trains to keep out of the way of the faster passenger services. Even so, 7A09 left Merehead more than two hours late that day and was still over an hour down when it reached this location.

Above right: This is a viewpoint that until the late spring of 2022 had not previously been available for photography. From Crofton Lock No. 56 to canal bridge No. 102 the land between the railway and the canal was occupied by a dense grove of Poplar trees. These had been planted in the early to mid-1960s and by the 1970s they completely obscured the track. After reaching a height of some 60 feet, only a few weeks before this photograph was taken, Network Rail cut the trees down on safety grounds as some had become rotten, opening up this view. Modern technology has also allowed an additional seven metres in height to be gained by the use of a photographic pole. On 7 June 2022, 59206 "John F Yeoman Rail Pioneer" climbs past the remains of the felled trees towards Wolfhall with 7Z60, the 11.15 Brentford–Merehead empties.

Right: The most intense spell of cold weather for more than ten years resulted in the Kennet and Avon Canal being frozen from bank to bank in late 2022. The canal was also devoid of boats as it had been closed to allow engineering work by the pumping station at Crofton, creating this scene where nothing disturbed the iced-over watercourse. On 15 December 2022, the low winter sunlight catches the frost-covered canal as GWR IET sets 802022 and 802010 twist their way through the reverse curves on their descent from Wolfhall to Crofton with 1A84, the 10.15 Penzance–Paddington.

Above: On 20 June 2022, 66594 "NYK Spirit of Kyoto" and 59201 bring 7A17, the 10.24 Merehead–Colnbrook, past the bridge abutments of the former M&SWJR independent avoiding line. This began from the southern side of the railway triangle mentioned in the caption for 37676 & 37685 on page 37, before passing above the Berks & Hants Line at this point and continuing north to Savernake High Level station. The layout of the lines in this area formed a network of some complexity, with two different lines initially heading away to the west from here. The GWR's Berks & Hants Line travelled west to Savernake Low Level and the M&SWJR's line used the adjacent Savernake High Level station. From Savernake, until 1933, two completely separate lines ran north from Savernake to Marlborough; these were the Marlborough Railway's 1864 branch which began from Savernake Low Level and the M&SWJR's 1898 independent avoiding line via Savernake High Level. Meanwhile, the B&HER's line continued west towards Pewsey and Devizes.

Above right: The Swindon Marlborough & Andover Railway (SM&AR) reached Marlborough from the north in 1881 and formed part of the M&SWJR's route to the south from 1884, when the company was created from the SM&AR and the Swindon & Cheltenham Extension Railway (S&CER). Until the independent avoiding line was built in 1898, the SM&AR and then the M&SWJR trains used the existing 1864 branch between Marlborough and Savernake Low Level, continuing over the Berks & Hants Line to Wolfhall, before the line continued south towards Tidworth and Andover by branching off to the left at a point in the background of this shot. Through trains from Cheltenham to Southampton commenced in 1891 upon completion of the route north of Swindon. In the mid-1980s it was still possible to easily access the abutments of the M&SWJR overbridge at Wolfhall from which 50003 "Temeraire" is seen passing with 1A61, the 11.35 Newquay–Paddington on 3 August 1985.

Right: Although legally obliged to allow M&SWJR trains to use its tracks from Marlborough to Wolfhall Junction via Savernake Low Level, the GWR employed obstructive tactics against what it regarded as a hostile competitor, whereby trains were sometimes delayed at the junction by Savernake Low Level for nearly two hours. In response, M&SWJR shareholders successfully sponsored a bill for the Marlborough & Grafton Railway (M&GR) to build an independent avoiding line from Marlborough, via a separate station at Savernake (High Level), with a bridge over the GWR's line. This would then rejoin the existing M&SWJR line at Wolfhall South Junction, just short of Grafton Curve Junction which was built a few years later with the curve to Grafton East Junction (see the map on page 5). The new line opened in 1898 and little over a year later the M&GR was absorbed into the M&SWJR. This photograph was taken on 7 June 1986, again from the abutments of the bridge that previously carried the M&SWJR. 50041 "Bulwark" snakes its way through the reverse curves, working hard hauling 1C38, the 11.35 Paddington–Paignton.

Below: 50045 "Achilles" passes Wolfhall with the 13.25 Paddington–Exeter St Davids empty stock working on 28 September 1985. This is where the junction of the M&SWJR's line from the south and the GWR's line was situated, in the area seen in the foreground, complete with an exchange siding and signal box to the right. The avoiding line, which passed over the GWR line where the rear of the train is, closed in 1960, two years after Savernake High Level station closed in 1958. The former M&SWJR route from Swindon Town to Ludgershall then closed as a through route in 1961, although freight from Savernake Low Level to the former GWR station in Marlborough continued until 1964.

Right: With Rosebay Willowherb growing in profusion on the site of the former Wolfhall Junction, 50049 "Defiance" rounds the curve hauling 1A46, the 09.12 Penzance–Paddington on 19 July 1986. Wolfhall signal box stood at the point on the extreme left, near the bridge. The photographer is standing between today's surviving Berks & Hants Line and where the M&SWJR tracks arrived from the south, merging with the Berks and Hants just before the bridge.

Below right: Less than a week before the winter solstice and the shadows are already encroaching on the tracks, even though it's only just past lunchtime. On 15 December 2022, 59101 "Village of Whatley" drifts downhill at Wolfhall with 6Z16, the 10.18 Whatley–Appleford. The course of the abandoned M&SWJR avoiding line is marked by the line of trees at the edge of the field on the right, with part of the site of Savernake High Level station being visible above the rear of the train. The location of the former Savernake Low Level station is out of sight, being situated round the corner where the train has just come from.

Above: Contrasting nicely with the green of the early summer foliage and the blue sky, 59201 climbs past signal UW69 at Wolfhall towing 7C64, the 15.26 Acton–Merehead empties on 23 June 2020. Some seven months after Freightliner became responsible for the Mendip Rail traffic and acquired this locomotive, it is still in the red livery of its former owner, with its DB Cargo markings crudely and none too effectively painted out. Note the commemorative bell that has been fitted above the cab windows.

Above right: On 12 September 2015, DRS' 57303 "Pride of Carlisle", which was on hire to First Great Western, powers a rare daytime empty sleeper stock movement over the Berks and Hants at Wolfhall. It is running as 5Z40, the 09.20 Penzance–Paddington, in connection with the launch of the new GWR franchise which involved a photoshoot at Paddington. This included the other sleeper set, which featured the first carriage to carry the new green GWR livery. It seems that this working crept under the radar, with very few enthusiasts noticing that it was running, as I've not seen any other photographs of it on the Berks and Hants Line.

Right: 73962 "Dick Mabbutt" and 73963 "Janice" head the return working of 1Z74, the 16.24 Paignton–Waterloo "The Herd of Wildebeeste" railtour past Wolfhall on 16 July 2016. A second pair of 73s, 73107 "Tracy" and 73128 "OVS Bulleid", are out of sight on the rear of the train. In BR days, the Class 73 electro-diesels rarely strayed far from the area in the south-east that was electrified with a third rail, as their 600 hp English Electric 4SRKT engines aren't suitable for extended use on main line duties. When they did work longer distances on diesel power, overheating was often a cause of failures. From 2013, the freight operator GB Railfreight had a batch of Class 73s re-engined as Class 73/9s, using 1600 hp MTU 8V 4000 R43L units. These can now be found working as far afield as Fort William hauling the Caledonian Sleeper services on the West Highland leg of their journeys to and from Euston. This was therefore a truly bizarre sight for someone whose first contact with the 73s was back in the 1970s, when they were a strictly Southern Region sight and any off-region excursions were massively newsworthy.

Above: On 24 August 1985, 56047 has just cleared Savernake Summit with empty wagons that are bound for Merehead. The Large Logo livery locomotive is on a short stretch of level track, while the rear of the train is still on the last section of 1 in 106 ascent. This is the site of Savernake Low Level station, an attractive country junction that closed in 1966, all traces of which have since been removed.

Below: During the 1980s BR's Western Region put together an unusual combination of coaches that was used as a loco-hauled passenger set. It predominantly consisted of spare Mark 3 HST coaches, with a Mark 1 full brake vehicle that had been converted to a generator car on one end and another barrier vehicle on the other. The generator was required to provide electric train supply (heating and air conditioning), as the Mark 3 coaches that formed HST sets had different electrical systems to standard Mark 3 stock. This meant that locomotives equipped with electric train supply, such as Class 47/4s and Class 50s, were unable to interface with HST stock. As the set was self-contained, any air-braked locomotive could haul it, although Class 47s and 50s were the usual traction. In this case the "no-heat" Class 47/0 47157 has the generator set in tow at Savernake with 1A40, the 10.32 Paignton–Paddington on 13 June 1987. The train is covering for an unavailable HST set, after it worked 2C10, the 09.10 Newton Abbot–Paignton earlier that day.

Above: On 14 July 2021, 66541 and 59201 reach Savernake Summit with 6A74, the 08.58 Whatley–Theale, a working that on this occasion was running as a Class 6 train. It is passing the western portal of Bruce Tunnel, which is to the right of 66541. The footpath on the left descends to an underpass, before it travels beneath the railway and to the canal which is hidden in a cutting. The canal tunnel marks the summit of the Kennet and Avon and also of the railway which passes above it. Savernake signal box was located to the right, slightly behind the photographer. The box and the refuge siding it controlled were closed in 1978, by which time it was only open on summer Saturdays when traffic levels were heavier.

Right: Back in the days when a pole wasn't required to photograph the line here at Savernake, on 14 June 1986, 50001 "Dreadnought" powers up the bank in charge of 1A46, the 09.12 Penzance–Paddington. On the hill in the upper right area, the courses of the two former lines to Marlborough can be seen as the two parallel lines of trees. The M&SWJR became part of the GWR with the 1923 Grouping and the GWR then simplified some of the infrastructure between Marlborough and Wolfhall in 1933. This included connecting the GWR's Marlborough branch to the M&SWJR's adjacent line to Marlborough at a point two miles north of Savernake, so that the GWR line could be closed north of the new connection. A short section of the now-unnecessary duplicate line, at the northern end of the original GWR route, was retained to provide local freight facilities and this was accessed by way of a reversal from the former M&SWJR's Marlborough station.

Chapter 4 – Savernake to Fairwood Junction, Westbury

Above: HST power car 43190 leads 1C79, the 11.00 Paddington–Plymouth past Brimslade Farm on 21 February 2015. Brimslade lies between Burbage Wharf and the village of Wootton Rivers on the longer and steeper western side of Savernake Bank. It was originally intended for Savernake Low Level station to be located at Burbage Wharf, which is on the main Marlborough to Tidworth road, but the line's engineer advised otherwise. Burbage Goods Station was built at the Wharf and a siding and goods shed were provided for freight interchange with the adjacent canal until this closed in 1947.

Above right: On 20 September 2021, 59104 "Village of Great Elm" slowly climbs the 1 in 198 section of Savernake Bank as it passes Brimslade Farm with a fully laden 7A09, the 07.12 Merehead–Acton, which consists of 42 wagons and grosses at over 4000 tonnes. The 59s are fitted with "Super Series" wheel creep control, which uses doppler radar to compare ground speed with wheel rotation speed in order to minimise wheel slip. Even with that in operation, by this point the locomotive's speed is much less than the maximum permitted speed of 45 mph for a Class 7 freight, as it has been climbing for nearly seven miles after making a standing start out of Woodborough Loop. The high ground in the right background is Martinsell Hill. At 948 feet above sea level, this is the third highest point in Wiltshire and the site of an Iron Age hill fort.

Right: On 26 May 2023, there were two Class 59s on 7A09, the 07.12 Merehead–Acton rather than the usual Class 66/59 combination, although only the front loco was powering the train. 59203 leads 59101 "Village of Whatley" as it climbs towards Savernake at Wootton Rivers. It was a close run thing with 802019 nearly blocking my view of the freight train. The IET is racing west with 1C74, the 09.04 Paddington–Newquay. Another photographer was standing to the left of the large Rhododendron bush and he was less fortunate!

Above: 66151 bursts out from under the bridge at Wootton Rivers in charge of 4Z58, the 11.40 Oxford Banbury Road–Westbury empties on 25 February 2022. After a couple of hours at Westbury, the empty wagons were taken further west on the next stage of their journey to Machen Quarry in South Wales. This aggregate flow from Machen Quarry to Oxford was a temporary arrangement while Tytherington Quarry was closed for maintenance, running instead of the usual workings from Tytherington to Appleford. 66151 looks like it hasn't had the benefit of a wash since it was used on the previous autumn's Berks and Hants Rail Head Treatment Trains. This is the site of Wootton Rivers Halt, which was opened by the GWR in 1928. One of many such small wayside stations, its intended purpose was a means of competition with the local bus services, but it would be closed just 38 years later in 1966.

Above right: On 6 July 2022, 66555 leads 59201 past Victory Bridge, which is just east of Pewsey, on 7A09, the 07.12 Merehead–Acton. With the 75 mph-geared Class 66 leading, both locomotives will need to be under power to cope with the weight being hauled. The train is just coming onto level track after having climbed the 1 in 260 gradient out of the Pewsey Dip. This will be the last relief it has on the 18-mile section from Lavington to Savernake Summit.

Right: Manningford Bruce is about a mile west of Pewsey. This part of the Berks and Hants Line is much straighter, as the curves enforced by following the Kennet and Avon Canal no longer feature after the railway parts from the canal at Wootton Rivers (when heading west). The GWR opened Manningford Halt at this location in 1932, but like many other rural stations, it didn't survive the 1960s as it was closed in 1966. 59103 "Village of Mells" heads west across the open countryside with 7V60, the 11.16 Brentford–Merehead empties on 24 February 2022. Less than a month after the line here opened, a head-on collision was narrowly avoided near Pewsey on 2 December 1862. The single track line was worked on the wooden staff and ticket system whereby no train should enter a single line section without holding the staff or being issued with a ticket and having seen the staff. There was no electric telegraph for communications between stations and in the line's early days the only passing place between Hungerford and Devizes was at Savernake. A westbound freight had departed Savernake with the staff instead of a ticket by mistake, and on arrival at Devizes the locomotive was sent back to Savernake bearing the staff. Meanwhile, a westbound passenger train had departed Savernake with the permission of the stationmaster, to avoid having to wait two hours for the next scheduled service from Devizes to return the staff. By sheer luck, men working on the line spotted the eastbound light engine and the train approaching from opposite direction, and managed to warn the drivers just in time, avoiding a catastrophe.

Above: Following the temporary downturn in passenger traffic caused by the Covid Pandemic, the passenger operator GWR gave up some of the GWML timetable paths that had previously caused the Theale to Robeston empty tanks to be routed via the Berks and Hants Line. From 8 August 2022, these reverted to being routed via Reading, Didcot and Swindon. During the last week they were seen on the Berks and Hants route, Class 66s were in use with a lighter load than usual, due to ten Class 60s being out of service awaiting mechanical attention at Toton. On 1 August 2022, 66094 is seen at Manningford Bruce with 6B33, the 13.35 Theale–Robeston which only consists of 14 bogie tanks.

Above right: 66158 is working well within its limits hauling 6Z25, the moderately-loaded 09.14 Westbury–Cricklewood, as it heads towards the western of the two overbridges at Manningford Bruce on 8 August 2022. On this occasion, the train didn't have to stop in Woodborough Loop and it is now descending the gentle gradient towards the Pewsey Dip. There is no danger of trains unexpectedly creeping up on you at this location, as the railway is intersected by several foot crossings for the local public footpaths and the drivers sound the horn as they approach each of these.

Right: There are passing loops in both directions at Woodborough and as the next passing point is 15 miles to the west in Westbury, the loops are frequently used to allow high speed passenger trains to overtake freight workings. 60039 "Dove Holes" approaches the junction for the Down loop with 6B33, the 13.35 Theale–Robeston empty tanks on 17 March 2022. 6B33 was booked to spend eight minutes in the loop, but as it was running nearly half an hour early on this occasion, it was allowed to miss its scheduled stop there and continue down the main line. At Heywood Road Junction it will leave the Berks and Hants by taking a right hand turn, and proceeding north through Hawkeridge Junction towards Bath.

Above: This busy morning scene at Woodborough on 29 September 2023 sees 59102 "Village of Chantry" draw 6C29, the 07.15 Willesden–Merehead empties into the Down loop, while 59206 "John F Yeoman Rail Pioneer" waits in the Up loop with a very short 6A09, the 07.12 Merehead–Acton. Meanwhile, Network Rail staff have just arrived to give some attention to the yellow USP 6000 Ballast Regulator that be can be seen in the sidings and only a few seconds after this photograph was taken a Paddington-bound IET unit passed by.

Above right: On 20 September 2021, 59001 "Yeoman Endeavour" passes the site of the former Patney and Chirton station with 6M20, the 10.38 Whatley–Churchyard Sidings. From this angle, it is difficult to imagine a station was ever here. The photograph was taken from the former station's footbridge, which survives to carry a public footpath over the line. The main platform was on the left with the buildings behind the photographer and there was an island platform in the area buried in vegetation on the right, the outer face of which served trains to and from Devizes. The original Berks and Hants Extension Railway from Hungerford to Devizes swung away to the right (north-west) at a junction to the west of this location. The surviving line beyond this junction was built by the GWR as the Stert-Westbury cutoff, as part of the scheme to provide a shorter route from Paddington to the West Country which is mentioned in the introduction. This faster line was completed in 1900, which was when Patney and Chirton station opened as the new junction for the original B&HER line to Devizes. The station and the 1862-built line to Devizes were both closed in 1966, along with the other intermediate stations between Great Bedwyn and Westbury, with the exception of Pewsey.

Right: On 8 August 2022, 66531 sweeps round the curve at Great Cheverell, which is approximately six miles west of Patney and Chirton, at the head of 6M20, the 10.38 Whatley–Churchyard Sidings. The locomotive is beginning the 18-mile ascent to Savernake Summit on a stretch that climbs for over five miles at 1 in 222.

Above: This colourful view was captured from the bridge seen in the background of the previous photograph. On 20 September 2021, 59203 brings 7C77, the 12.41 Acton–Merehead empties around Great Cheverell curve. Great Cheverell never had its own station as Lavington was only about a mile to the east. The station there opened in 1900 and closed in 1966, although its goods yard hung on into 1967.

Above right: Several different grades of aggregate are processed at and shipped out of the Mendip quarries. The finer products can produce the effect seen here, especially if the train is running as a Class 6 working, which has a 60 mph speed limit, as opposed to the 45 mph limit of a Class 7 train. Creating quite a dust storm, 59002 "Alan J Day" leans into the start of Great Cheverell Curve with 6L21, the 13.23 Whatley–Dagenham on 7 September 2021.

Right: 66605 is seen from Baynton bridge near Edington early in the morning of 14 July 2022. It is travelling on the predominantly straight and almost level seven-mile section that runs east from Heywood Road Junction at Westbury, hauling 6A82, the 04.37 Whatley–Hayes & Harlington. Edington and Bratton station used to exist about a mile west of here, but was an early casualty, closing to passenger traffic in 1952. Its signal box closed in 1959 and it then closed to freight in 1963.

Right: On a hot and hazy summer Saturday of 27 August 1983, we find 50021 "Rodney" in charge of 1B66, the 11.15 Paddington–Paignton. It is travelling on the Westbury avoiding line, which bypasses the Wiltshire town by skirting south on the line that runs for more than two miles between Heywood Road and Fairwood Junctions. It has just passed under the line from Westbury to Warminster and Salisbury. The Westbury avoiding line was opened in 1933, after the GWR took advantage of the Developments (Loan Guarantees and Grants) Act of 1929. The Act was passed to finance public works in order to decrease unemployment and the GWR utilised it to improve facilities at many locations, including construction of the avoiding lines here and at nearby Frome.

Below: On 8 August 2022, 66605 approaches Fairwood Junction on the original line through Westbury station hauling 6C48, the 12.49 Appleford–Whatley empties. This service had been routed to run via Didcot, Swindon, Chippenham, Melksham and Trowbridge. Having arrived from the Trowbridge direction, it had no choice but to use this line, however the freight trains routed along the Berks and Hants Line can be more unpredictable. Being booked to use the avoiding line or that via Westbury station is no guarantee that a particular freight service will do so, with changes taking place at short notice depending on traffic regulation or crew change requirements. All too often one can stand here, or on the bridge just the other side of the field on the right, only to have to make a mad dash between the two, or see the intended photographic target pass by a hundred yards away!

Right: This unusual combination sees NSE-liveried 47573 "The London Standard" hauling the two DMU sets that form the 16.08 Bristol–Weymouth. The train is seen near Fairwood Junction on 6 August 1988. By the late 1980s, reliability of the 30-year-old first generation DMUs

was becoming increasingly poor and it is assumed that a fault led to these sets having to be loco-hauled. Earlier that day I'd photographed the same DMUs being hauled by 47560 "Tamar" on the outward working, the 13.05 Weymouth–Bristol. The Westbury White Horse can clearly be seen on the hillside in the background. This was reputedly created to commemorate King Alfred's victory over the Danes at the Battle of Ethandun in 878; there is however, no evidence of its existence before 1772 and the current horse dates from 1778.

Below: This was the same view almost exactly 34 years later. Although HSTs were an everyday sight on the Berks and Hants Line until 2019, those operated by the Cross Country franchise were not, especially in this formation with two power cars coupled back to back. On 8 August 2022, 43301 and 43285 are seen approaching Fairwood Junction near Westbury with 5Z43, the 08.20 Laira–Laira. The short train is a route learning special, preparing Cross Country drivers for planned diversions. It had travelled from Plymouth to Bristol Temple Meads via Cogload Junction, Westbury and Bath before retracing its steps in the opposite direction.

Above: 56034 "Castell Ogwr/Ogmore Castle" swings left at Fairwood Junction as it takes the line for Westbury station on 6 August 1988. The wagons appear to be carrying Tarmac branding so this is likely to be a Frome North Yard–Hothfield working. The locomotive was new to traffic in August 1977, later being withdrawn from service in 1999 and it was scrapped by C F Booth of Rotherham in November 2007.

Below: Taken from the same location almost 34 years later, 59203 heads straight through Fairwood Junction and onto the Westbury avoiding line on 14 July 2022. It is hauling 6A74, the 08.58 Whatley–Theale, over the switched diamond at slow speed because a restriction was in place due to the warm weather. Note that the sides of the rails have been painted white to help reflect sunlight. Network Rail staff were onsite to monitor proceedings that day, although temperatures only reached about 24C. They almost touched 40C the following week though, which meant that there was a genuine risk of the rails buckling.

Below: 66604 heads away from Westbury station and approaches Fairwood Junction with the rake of empty box wagons that forms 6C68, the 11.38 Avonmouth–Whatley on 7 September 2021. The 2 mile 37-chain avoiding line can be seen on the right as it also approaches the junction. The distance via the avoiding line is actually 1 chain (22 yards) longer than the original route, but the station area is speed restricted, so it still offers a time saving.

Below: 33051 brings 2V23, the 08.58 Weymouth–Bristol Temple Meads through Fairwood Junction prior to its booked stop at Westbury on 3 October 1987. Back in the 1970s this view was enhanced by the signal box that used to stand to the right of the pointwork and the mature Elm trees that were behind it. The signal box was demolished following the completion of the Westbury resignalling scheme in May 1984 and the Elms were felled after succumbing to the Dutch Elm Disease epidemic that swept the country in the 1970s.

Chapter 5 – Doubles & More

This chapter comprises a selection of photographs showing two or more locomotives working trains over the Berks and Hants Line. The use of more than one engine on the route is usually for one of three reasons; to provide enough power and brake force to work the train, to assist a failed locomotive, or to save a separate light engine movement having to be made. Regular double heading of passenger trains on the line hasn't been common since 1970, when the scheduled use of pairs of Class 42 Warship diesel-hydraulics ceased, but freight services have regularly featured pairs, especially following the demise of the Class 52 Western diesel-hydraulics which were ideally suited for the heavy aggregates traffic. In modern times, even though the Class 59s are more than capable of hauling even the heaviest freight trains over the line's most significant gradients, the use of multiple locomotives continues. Often only one of these works under power though, with the other(s) being towed.

Above: Even though they were descending at 1 in 175, the 12CSVT engines of 37211 and 37354 could be heard well before they came into view at Kennet and Avon Canal Bridge No. 99, as they headed east with loaded Yeoman box wagons on 22 June 1989. Following the final withdrawal of the Class 52 "Western" diesel-hydraulics in 1977, Foster Yeoman had wanted to purchase a small batch of these to operate privately with their own drivers, but opposition from the rail unions scuppered that plan. BR's answer was to utilise pairs of Class 37s on the Berks and Hants aggregate workings, providing greater engine and brake power than a single Type 4 locomotive could. Although Type 5 Class 56s had appeared on the route in numbers by the mid-1980s, 37s still continued to be seen.

Above: 66134 and 66192, both of which are clearly under power, descend towards Standers Foot Crossing near Hungerford with 6Z53, the 05.23 Tytherington–Appleford on 17 November 2021. While many modern day multiple locomotive workings are simply dead in tow movements to avoid using a light engine timetable path, this working was regularly double-headed like this. It is booked to run as a 2200-tonne load, but with 33 wagons in tow the actual weight would be above 3000 tonnes, which is beyond the limit of a standard 75 mph-geared Class 66 over Savernake Bank.

Above: 66054 and 66121 pass Little Bedwyn Lock No. 67 with 6Z54, the 05.13 Tytherington–Cricklewood on 15 June 2022. This working is part of the same flow as that in the previous photograph; Cricklewood was sometimes used as an alternative destination depending on where the HS2 project required the aggregate. With no paths available on the Great Western Main Line (GWML), the service was routed the long way round via Bristol, Bath and Westbury, then along the Berks and Hants Line. At the time of writing in 2023, DC Rail Freight are now responsible for the flow from Tytherington to Appleford, and since the GWR passenger franchise has relinquished a number of GWML passenger paths, these trains can now use the direct route via Swindon.

Above: 66134 and 66074 bring 6A53, the late running 05.13 Tytherington–Appleford up Savernake Bank at Wootton Rivers on 8 August 2022. After running through Heywood Road Junction at Westbury ten minutes early, 6A53 came to a stand on the Berks and Hants Line for some 30 minutes, apparently awaiting a crew change. This meant that the IETs following 6A53 had to sit and wait on the Westbury avoiding line and then crawl all the way to Woodborough before they could overtake the freight train!

Right: 6A53, the 05.13 Tytherington–Appleford is scheduled to spend an hour or so sitting in Hungerford Up Loop, which easily allows more than one shot of it to be taken at different locations should one wish to do so. 66041 and 66002 round Kintbury Curve as they work hard to accelerate away from Hungerford Up Loop on 10 October 2022.

Above: The transport of petroleum products has been a feature of the Berks and Hants Line for many years. Although there have been other flows of fuel over the route during the last 40 years, including that from Fawley to Aldermaston, the one that survives today is from Robeston in Pembrokeshire to the distribution depot at Theale, which is currently owned by Puma Energy. In mixed liveries, typical of the period, 37294 and 37078 bring 6A18, the 04.35 Robeston–Theale past Wolfhall on 22 June 1989.

Below: In the beautiful low autumnal light of 25 November 2022, 66551 leads 59203 under the bridge at Hungerford Common with a full length 7A09, the 07.12 Merehead–Acton. Both locomotives are under power, as with 42 wagons and more than 4000 tonnes in tow, 66551 would struggle on its own.

Above: 66558 and 59201 are seen just east of Crofton with 7A09, which on 11 July 2022 was running an hour early. The signallers were busy that day because Woodborough Up Loop was out of use due to the high temperatures causing heat stress on the rails. With 6A53, which was running as 6Z54 to Cricklewood that day, already occupying Hungerford Up Loop, 7A09 had to be out of the way at Theale before the IETs that followed were scheduled to reach there.

Below: We return to the BR days, when 37215 and 37221 were making a large amount of noise on Crofton Curve at the head of 6A18, the 04.35 Robeston–Theale on 14 April 1989. The load is 14 bogie tanks, some 10 less than the Class 60s now routinely handle. 37221 went on to have a spell in France working on one of the Ligne à Grande Vitesse (LGV) construction projects before returning to the UK; it was withdrawn in 2009 and was then cut up at C F Booths of Rotherham. 37215 has had a happier time though. Stored in 1992 and withdrawn in 1993, it was purchased for preservation by the Growler Group and can now be found operating on the Gloucestershire and Warwickshire Railway.

Right: 66566 and 59002 "Alan J Day" slowly grind past Manningford Bruce having just brought 7A09, the 07.12 Merehead–Acton out of the Up loop at Woodborough on 8 August 2022. Woodborough Loops are located on a rising gradient of 1 in 255, which means that loaded eastbound trains that stop there are faced with a standing start straight onto a climb of more than a mile before they reach the Pewsey dip.

Below: 66538 and 59002 "Alan J Day" come round the corner from Wolfhall as they carefully descend towards Crofton with 7A09, the 07.12 Merehead–Acton on 21 September 2022. Freightliner now double-heads 7A09 because Acton Yard is owned by DB Cargo; wanting to minimise the charges the company incurs, instead of stabling separate locomotives in Acton Yard to work the second portion of 7A09 forward, all the traction required travels on the train itself in this way. For operational reasons the Class 66 always seems to lead, which means that both locomotives have to be under power to handle the weight of a full load over Savernake Bank. If the Class 59 were to lead, it would happily take the train and the "dead" 66 by itself.

Above: On 7 June 1986, 47142 has a failed 50048 "Dauntless" and 1A42, the 10.30 Paignton-Paddington, in tow as it comes up the last few yards of the 1 in 132 climb to Savernake Summit. Class 50 availability was probably at its peak in 1986, with the refurbishment programme for the class having been completed in 1983 and this was just before sectorisation began to condemn the class to early withdrawal from 1987. This was the only instance of a Class 50 failure that I ever saw on the Berks and Hants Line, and that was from a very large number of sightings. On some summer Saturdays during 1986, Class 50s were hauling all of the locomotive-hauled passenger services that I saw on the route, as well as the empty newspaper vans from Plymouth.

Above right: 9 May 2015 saw diversions over the Berks and Hants Line, with the GWML closed for work at Reading, where the station rebuild was nearing completion. DB Schenker had a Saturday Q path (runs as required) in the timetable for steel traffic that had come through the Channel Tunnel from France. This would run from Dollands Moor to Margam and had become a very irregular and infrequent runner by 2015, so it was a real bonus to capture 6V13, the 08.12 Dollands Moor–Margam behind 66034 and 66096 from Bridge No. 99. The train was double headed to cope with the climb to Savernake summit.

Right: 66142, 66008 and 66140 form 0Z66, the 14.03 Margam–Didcot light engine convoy which is seen passing Great Bedwyn on 23 August 2014. The elderly GWR design of rail-built buffer stop in the forground survived here until the turnback siding was lengthened so that it could accommodate IET units. Ironically, most trains at Bedwyn are now once again worked by Turbo units which don't need the lengthened siding and these only provide a shuttle service to and from Newbury outside of the peak hours.

Above: 33047 and 33107 are working in multiple as they climb past Wolfhall with the rake of empty bogie ballast hoppers that forms 6V96, the 09.50 Tonbridge–Meldon on 14 April 1989. The lead locomotive has a steam-era 73A Stewarts Lane shed plate on the centre of its front end; this was one of many minor depot-led embellishments and livery variations that could be seen on the traction at the time.

Below: 59103 "Village of Mells" and 59102 "Village of Chantry" are seen from the same location at Wolfhall more than 31 years later on 23 June 2020. They are heading 7C77, the 12.41 Acton–Merehead empties. 7C77 is one of the principal afternoon westbound services that return the empty wagons to Merehead Quarry, and like the morning loaded 7A09, it almost always runs. It is usual to see multiple locomotives in the consist in order to save a timetable path to move engines back to the Mendips, but for some reason two Hanson-liveried Class 59s is not a combination I've seen very often.

Right: More than a year after the previous photograph was taken and 7C77 is still being double-headed, although the usual combination has now become a Class 66 leading a Class 59. The gallery of photographers that were gathered at Great Cheverell on 7 September 2021 were a little irritated to find the scruffy 66524 leading, with the freshly-repainted 59202 in a less conspicuous position on 7C77, the 12.41 Acton–Merehead empties.

Below: Reliability of the Class 60s has never been as good as that of the Class 59s and 66s, but this isn't really a fair comparison, as the General Motors units are the end product of development and feedback on many thousands of locomotives that had been built and improved upon over the years. The Class 60s, or Tugs as they are known to many, are a class of just 100 locomotives that were built with no effective prototype or predecessor, and with a much higher use of electronics than previous classes; many of their early teething problems were software-related. During the warm summers of 2020 to 2022, especially 2022 when temperatures approached 40 degrees at times on the Berks and Hants Line, it became apparent that the Class 60s did not agree with high temperatures, as a number of failures were noted. In this case, 60015 failed on the Robeston–Theale circuit twice in one week. On the second occasion it was rescued by 66106 at Theale and the pair are seen just west of Great Bedwyn with 6B33, the 13.35 Theale–Robeston empties on 25 June 2020.

Above left: 66514 and 59103 "Village of Mells" bring 7C77, the 12.41 Acton–Merehead empties, around Crofton Curve on 21 October 2021. Acton Yard had been the nexus of the Mendip aggregates traffic in London for decades, but after Freightliner took over the Mendip Rail contract in November 2019, the company had to start paying DB Cargo to access the latter's infrastructure there. For the first two years, only minor modifications were made to Freightliner's operations, but as the next photograph illustrates, that was about to change.

Left: On 17 March 2022, 7C77 approaches Woodborough Loops when this working had become the 12.22 Wembley–Merehead empties. By this time, Freightliner had reduced its use of Acton Yard to a minimum, with only 7A09 still calling there to split into its constituent portions. The other major operational change can be seen here; instead of the train formation having the second locomotive behind the leading engine, the rear loco has simply been coupled to the back with its separate portion of wagons still attached. 59204 is at the head of 7C77 and 66569 is dead in tow half-way down the train with the empty JHA hoppers that it had brought to Wembley.

Above: Modern day Mendip Rail operations can result in triple heading when locomotives need to be returned to Merehead or Whatley. Although carrying spare locomotives half-way down the train has now become the norm, 59005 "Kenneth J Painter", 66539 and 66555 have reverted to the traditional mode of operation on 27 June 2022. The trio are seen just west of Fairfield Foot Crossing with 7C77, the 12.19 Wembley–Merehead empties.

Above: Triple-heading of locomotives occurs on occasion these days, but quadruple-heading is particularly unusual on the Berks and Hants Line. 20 June 2022 saw 59101 "Village of Whatley", 59203, 66416 and 59204 all attached to the front of 7C77, the 12.19 Wembley–Merehead empties. In this case, the third and fourth locomotives, 66416 and 59204, were being moved west with 7C77 to save on light engine timetable paths, while 59203 was being returned to Merehead for mechanical attention after it had failed.

Below: In 1985, BR-era aggregate operations on the Berks and Hants Line usually relied on a single Class 47 or Class 56, or double-headed Class 37s, so seeing this combination appear round the corner at Wolfhall on 28 September 1985 was a jaw dropping surprise! 56050, 56048 and the unique 47901 are seen heading west with a rake of empty box wagons.

Chapter 6 – Steam Specials

The Berks and Hants Line has always proved popular with the organisers of steam-hauled railtours. The lower traffic density, especially at weekends when there is less freight scheduled, means that finding paths for steam-hauled services with a maximum speed of 60 or 75mph is easier than on busier lines. It also includes the challenge of Savernake Bank, meaning the locomotives can be heard working hard, which is popular with passengers and photographers. This chapter presents a selection of steam-worked trains seen on the Berks and Hants over the years.

Above: Southern Railway Battle of Britain Class 4-6-2 34067 "Tangmere" passes the exit of the Down Towney Loop at Lower Padworth with 1Z27, The Railway Touring Company's "Somerset Explorer" railtour on 14 February 2009. This ran as the 09.20 Paddington–Yeovil Junction, which travelled via Reading, Castle Cary and Yeovil, with the return leg running via Salisbury, Basingstoke and Southcote Junction. This was a busy day for steam photography, as 60163 "Tornado" was making its first run in the south of England, also visiting Salisbury, albeit avoiding the station on Laverstock Curve.

Above: When steam hauled, the Belmond British Pullman has long been associated with rebuilt Merchant Navy Class 4-6-2 35028 "Clan Line". On 13 June 2012, the well-known locomotive was captured passing Crofton alongside the moored canal boat "Levick" with 1Z91, the 08.45 London Victoria–Bristol Temple Meads.

Above right: Early morning steam locomotive movements over the Berks and Hants Line are quite rare; usually railtours starting from or near to London will reach the Crofton area around mid-morning. In this case, Class A4 4-6-2 60007 "Sir Nigel Gresley" was travelling with its support coach from Southall to Taunton, where it would take over from 47237 on 1Z32, the 07.51 Guildford–Kingswear "Dartmouth Express" on 19 April 2014. With the temperature near freezing and not a breath of wind, conditions were near perfect, allowing an undisturbed reflection in the canal, as seen from beneath Bridge No. 99. That is embellished by an ethereal hint of mist on the water's surface and an epic plume of exhaust, despite the fact that 60007 was barely having to do any work with such a light load.

Right: By 2012 this was about as close to the classic Little Bedwyn view (as seen in the photo of 47623 on page 20) that was still possible. Today, the hedge between the canal and railway is taller than the bridge that this was taken from! On 21 July 2012, the crew of Battle of Britain Class 4-6-2 34067 "Tangmere" take in the vista as they pass with 1Z44, the 08.04 Paddington–Minehead "West Somerset Steam Express" railtour.

Above: On an atmospheric 22 October 2016, beside the Kennet and Avon Canal at Kintbury, we see LMS Princess Royal Class 4-6-2 6201 "Princess Elizabeth" heading west with 1Z46, the 07.14 Paddington–Minehead "West Somerset Steam Express" railtour. The locomotive played a part in the Diamond Jubilee celebrations for Queen Elizabeth II on 3 June 2012. After arriving in London with a railtour from Tyseley, 6201 was positioned on Battersea Railway Bridge and its whistle signalled the start of the Thames Diamond Jubilee Pageant.

Below: Crofton Lock No. 60, which is below the nearby pumping station, is always a popular spot for photographers when a steam-hauled railtour is running, as it has a picturesque view and the 1 in 183 gradient means the engine will be working hard. Double headed steam is certainly not an everyday sight on the Berks and Hants Line, so quite a crowd had gathered to watch Class 5MT "Black 5" 4-6-0 44871 and Class N15 King Arthur Class 4-6-0 30777 "Sir Lamiel" power up the hill at Crofton towards Savernake Summit with 1Z27, the 08.06 Paddington–Weymouth "Royal Wessex" railtour on 22 May 2010.

Above: On 26 June 2010, King Class 4-6-0 6024 "King Edward I" nears Bridge No. 99 with 1Z27, the late-running 09.07 Paddington–Exeter St Davids "Cornish Riviera Express" railtour. It turned out to be an eventful day for those travelling on this train. At Colthorp, near Theale, a fire on the generator car caused a lengthy delay, then as can be seen from the exhaust, poor steaming made things worse. Ultimately, 6024 had to be assisted by D1015 "Western Champion", which was brought into action earlier than planned, providing assistance from Taunton to Exeter. There, Castle Class 4-6-0 5029 "Nunney Castle" was attached to form a steam double header as far as Par, with D1015 then taking over for the run to Penzance in line with the schedule. For the return leg, 5029 and 6024 double headed the lengthy return working from Penzance to Paddington as originally intended.

Below: The Railway Touring Company's annual "Great Britain" railtour was, and still is, quite an event in the steam haulage calendar, as it makes a lengthy journey across the United Kingdom over a number of days. The 2011 "Great Britain IV" covered more ground than most, reaching destinations as far afield as Wick and Thurso on the Far North line and Penzance at the opposite end of the country. On 24 April 2011, during the final leg of the train's long journey, Castle Class 4-6-0 5029 "Nunney Castle" drops down from Savernake at Wolfhall with 1Z68, the 11.00 Bristol Temple Meads–Paddington.

Right: In contrast to 2011, the "Great Britain XV" traversed the Berks and Hants Line in the opposite direction on its opening day in 2023. Class 5MT "Black Five" 4-6-0 44932 approaches Crofton alongside the Kennet and Avon Canal with 1Z10, the 07.11 Paddington–Plymouth on 15 April 2023. 44932 was substituting for the rebuilt Merchant Navy Class 35018 "British India

Line", which was originally scheduled to haul the train but was unavailable. As the Black Five was less powerful than the Merchant Navy, diesel 47802 was attached to the rear of the train to provide assistance if necessary, but there was no indication of it being used here and 44932 was working very hard.

Below: 60103 "Flying Scotsman" attracts massive public interest when it runs on the national network, especially since completion of its extremely expensive ten-year restoration in 2016. Sometimes this goes too far, with incidents of railway trespass often associated with the locomotive's appearances. Westbound afternoon steam hauled services on the Berks and Hants Line are extremely rare, so the opportunity was taken to photograph the Class A3 4-6-2 at Hungerford Common on 25 August 2019, when it worked a circular route. Beginning at Paddington, it ran via High Wycombe, Bicester and Oxford, before proceeding south to Reading and onto the Berks & Hants route, then skirting north at Westbury it continued to Oxford via Melksham and Swindon. The excursion then finished with a final run to Paddington. This leg was running as 1Z05, the 14.15 Newbury Racecourse–Oxford Parkway.

Above: With the Gresley three-cylinder syncopated exhaust beat filling the air, Class A4 4-6-2 60009 "Union of South Africa" is attacking the gradient towards Crofton at Bridge No. 99 at the head of 1Z69, the 09.54 London Victoria–Bristol Temple Meads "Cathedrals Express" railtour on 1 December 2007. Built in 1937 and withdrawn from BR service in June 1966, 60009 was quickly preserved. From 1989 it started working railtours on the national rail network until its main line career ended in March 2020. The engine was steamed for the last time in September 2021 and is now a static exhibit.

Below: Class A1 4-6-2 60163 "Tornado" was completed in 2008, becoming the first new standard gauge main line steam locomotive to be built in the UK since 1960. Its first visit to the Berks and Hants was on 18 June 2009, when it hauled the "Sunny South Special" railtour from London Victoria–Minehead and back under the "Cathedrals Express" brand. The return working, 1Z95, the 16.05 Minehead–Victoria came to a stand near Somerton with an air pump problem and lost around 20 minutes before getting underway again. With further delays for operational reasons, the train eventually passed Wolfhall, as shown here, 45 minutes late. That turned out to be fortunate for the photographers who were gathered here, because at its scheduled time it was extremely dark here, with heavy cloud overhead. The sun started to appear as we heard "Tornado" reach Savernake Summit, then came out only seconds before it passed by, before vanishing for good while we walked back to the car!

Chapter 7 – Boats

To the west of Newbury, the railway closely follows the course of the Kennet and Avon Canal, particularly between Kintbury and Wolfhall, providing many photographic locations where trains and the canal can be captured together. Sometimes boats can be incorporated into the scene, either moored at the canal side, in a lock, or more rarely, moving on the water as a train passes by. As mentioned in the captions, I had to wait a very long time before I was fortunate enough to capture a moving boat and a train together.

Above: Before the Kennet and Avon was fully restored in 1990, boats were much less frequently seen moving up and down the canal. Vessels are more common today, but I still had to wait 37 years before finally capturing a moving boat and train in the same photograph! Looking as though it could be a GWR publicity picture, IET 802018 forms 1A74, the 07.13 Paignton–Paddington, as it passes Crofton Pumping Station while a boat approaches Crofton Lock No. 61 on 12 August 2020.

Above right: On 24 August 1985, 50045 "Achilles" hauls 1C51, the 14.15 Paddington–Paignton through Crofton with the small cabin cruiser "Tolza" moored up on the Kennet and Avon. Although the canal can accommodate widebeam boats, most craft viewed on it today tend to be traditional canal boats of varying widths. Cruisers such as this are not seen quite as much, at least not on the section paralleled by the railway.

Right: This view looking back at Crofton Lock No. 61 sees a busy scene on 15 June 2022, with one boat moored up, another coming through the lock and 59202 passing with 6C31, the 10.08 Theale–Whatley empties. The photograph was taken from a height of seven metres using a pole, while another photographer who is also using a pole is visible on Canal Bridge No. 100.

Above: 66526 "Driver Steve Dunn (George)" and 59206 "John F Yeoman Rail Pioneer" take 7C77, the 12.41 Acton–Merehead empties past Froxfield Bottom Lock No. 70 on 10 August 2021. A boater travelling in the other direction is operating the gates while widebeam boat "Silver Tree" enters the lock.

Above right: 59206 "John F Yeoman Rail Pioneer" passes a boat heading towards Bridge No. 99 with 7A09, the 07.12 Merehead–Acton near Crofton on 23 July 2021. After decades of decay and neglect, the dilapidated canal bridge had been restored during 2017 by military veterans from the Heritage Heroes project, along with the Canal and Rivers Trust. The work involved repairing the brickwork, installing new parapets and improving access.

Right: On 29 September 2021, 66020 and its rake of loaded box wagons form 6M15, the 07.07 Tytherington–Calvert HS2 aggregate working. This was the final week for deliveries to Calvert before HS2 construction work required removal of the unloading facilities there. From the following Monday, only a few engineering trains from Hinksey Yard near Oxford visited Calvert, until the lifting of the track back to Quainton Road was completed.

Above: 66542 with 6C58, the 11.45 Oxford Banbury Road–Whatley empties approaches Crofton Pumping Station alongside Crofton Lock No. 60, while a family waits for their holiday boat to enter the lock on 24 August 2021.

Above right: A boat gently descends within Crofton Lock No. 57 as a First Great Western HST set led by power car 43196 leads a westbound service in the opposite direction on 4 September 2013. 43196 would be retired in 2019, before being scrapped by Sims Metal in Newport during December 2022. The parapet for the Grafton curve bridge over the canal is hidden in the undergrowth beyond the person sitting on the lock gate, where the tree overhangs the canal.

Right: While forming 1C82, the 13.24 Paddington–Plymouth on 20 June 2022, IET set 802103 winds around the reverse curves between Crofton and Wolfhall, beside Crofton Lock No. 56, while the owner of "Amica" opens the paddles on the lock gates to descend towards the pumping station. All the trees between the canal and railway had recently been felled, except for this solitary survivor; prior to that, the last time this view of the canal and railway was available was when the Berks and Hants was dominated by diesel-hydraulics, although at that time the canal was derelict. It probably wasn't since commercial traffic on the Kennet and Avon disappeared in the early 1950s, that a photograph of a boat and train together was last possible here. As of Spring 2023, this view is again no longer possible, as new Poplar saplings were planted to replace the felled trees.

Chapter 8 – Weather & Light

Above: On 29 February 2020, a cold front moving in from the west brought a belt of heavy rain with thunderstorms on the trailing edge. Clearer air followed behind, giving views such as this, while the bad weather receded into the distance. 165121 heads for its scheduled stop at Hungerford forming 2K15, the 14.27 Newbury–Bedwyn, with a huge towering cumulonimbus cloud providing the backdrop.

Above right: A similar weather combination occurred on 3 August 1985, giving a bright start before rain arrived from the west during the morning. With the clouds moving away to the east and a sunny afternoon now developing, 47014 takes a rake of empty ARC branded PGA hoppers past the disused M&SWJR overbridge abutments at Wolfhall.

Right: Low sunlight reflecting off the subject of a photograph can give an attractive golden glint if caught at the right angle. With the online resources that are available today, such as websites that confirm exactly where the sun will be shining from at a given location at a set time, planning shots like this is an easy task. Some of the best subjects for this type of photography are slab-sided modern passenger stock, as the lack of surface detail gives an almost liquid gold effect, as can be seen here. IET 800005 traverses Crofton Curve with 1A71, the 05.49 Plymouth–Paddington on 22 November 2021.

Above: Cold frosty mornings often produce good photographs and if the air is still enough scenes such as this are possible. With the temperature around freezing, a perfectly calm morning has allowed a layer of mist to form close to the surface of the slightly warmer canal. 66130 casts a reflection onto the waters as it passes with 6W05, a Westbury–Dolphin Junction (near Slough) engineering train on 19 April 2014.

Above right: During the periods just after sunrise and just before sunset, the sun's light has to penetrate the earth's atmosphere for a greater distance, due to the low angle of the sun. This scatters and reduces the intensity of the blue light, producing a reddish, golden hue which is known as the golden hour. Railway photography during such periods is rewarding, but finding suitable shadow-free locations when the sun is so low in the sky can be a challenge. 66136 and 66130 catch the early morning light at Hungerford Common while in charge of 6A53, the 05.23 Tytherington–Appleford on 7 February 2022. As it was booked to use the loop visible behind 66136, I had setup here, because the sun was high enough to illuminate all that track. Frustratingly, after setting the route into the loop, the signaller then changed the points for the train to pass by on the main line, where the shadows were still covering the ground. 66136 bears branding for the first through freight train to run from Yiwu in China to London in January 2017 and the return run in April of that year.

Right: On an absolutely bone-numbingly cold day at Crofton, the Kennet and Avon Canal has frozen from bank to bank. A light dusting of snow has fallen and the wind has blown this into streamers across the ice. Led by power car 43165 "Prince Michael of Kent", a First Great Western HST set heads for the West Country on 27 November 2010. I'd gone out to see the Theale to Robeston empty tanks, as they were due to be diverted over the Berks and Hants that Saturday. After losing the feeling in my feet while I waited for two hours, an email came through saying that 6B33 had been cancelled!

Above: On the morning of 12 January 2022, whilst the sun has melted the frost on the fields, most of the canal still remains in the shadows. Without a breath of wind, the water reflects the boats and surrounding trees at Crofton as 66165 powers past with 6Z25, the 09.16 Westbury–Cricklewood.

Above right: Digital photography has the advantage over physical film that a choice can be made after taking the shot as to whether the final result will be colour or black and white. Sometimes a monochrome image produces a more dramatic result. Processed in Photoshop to be a black and white image, as though a red filter had been used, has emphasised the patches of blue sky by darkening them and enhancing the lock's decaying brickwork. 43137 "Newton Abbot 150" brings up the rear of 1C77, the 10.06 Paddington–Penzance at Crofton Lock No. 57 on 1 April 2017.

Right: On 10 August 2021 the evening shadows lengthen, highlighting the furrows in the field alongside Beech Drive Crossing while 59205 approaches hauling 6C53, the 16.41 Acton–Merehead empties. Summertime sees perfect lighting at some locations where the sun would be on the wrong side of the line or backlit in winter; this is because the morning and evening sun rises and sets more to the north-east and north-west respectively during the lighter months.

Above: I was cutting it about as fine as possible with this image, to get the maximum golden hour effect. On 15 December 2022, 59103 "Village of Mells" takes in the last light of the day between Crofton and Wolfhall with a short 7C77, the 12.20 Wembley–Merehead empties. The chimney of Crofton Pumping Station can be seen in the background, above the rear of the train. I had hoped to get a shot of the train alongside the sunlit, frozen and frost-covered canal, but 7C77 was running nearly an hour late and the shadows were creeping further and further towards the tracks. A westbound IET was following this train, just two signalling blocks behind, but by the time it reached here the tracks were completely hidden in the shadows.

Above: Under a dramatic sky 66520 is about to cross Standers Foot Crossing with 6A60, the 08.32 Whatley–Oxford Banbury Road on 1 November 2021. As I took this photograph, a series of heavy showers were approaching from the west. With the rain heading towards me and this location being a good ten-minute walk from the car, a hasty exit was made once this view had been captured!

Above: With a threatening cloudscape and a weak patch of sunshine lightening the foreground, 60040 "The Territorial Army Centenary" brings 6B33, the 13.35 Theale–Robeston empty tanks past Crofton Lock No. 56 on 27 June 2022. This was the last occasion I photographed a Tug hauling 6B33 over the Berks and Hants Line before it was re-routed back onto the GWML via Reading.

Right: A foggy start to a late summer Saturday ensured the Kennet and Avon Canal was calm enough for a nearly-perfect reflection beside Bridge No. 99. 50017 "Royal Oak" passes with 1C25, the 09.40 Paddington–Penzance on 28 September 1985. The angled brick courses that make up the skew arch of this bridge are clearly visible here.

Chapter 9 – Autumn

Autumn is always a favourite time of year for railway photography. The unrelieved green of the foliage in the summer months gives way to golds and reds, and the sun no longer reaches so high in the sky, offering softer lighting. Some extra variety in the train services also appears, as the Rail Head Treatment Trains (RHTT) operate during leaf-fall season to help keep the track clear of leaf debris.

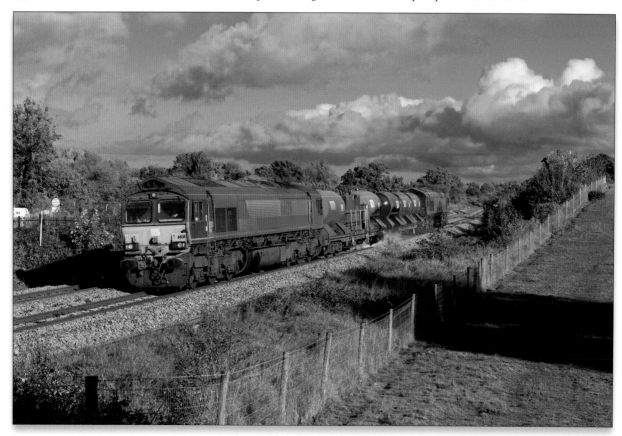

Above: The RHTT season usually begins around mid to late-October, depending on the state of leaf fall from the lineside trees. The equipment on the designated trains uses a high-pressure water jet to spray the track, which removes the leaf mulch that can soon become compressed onto the rails by the weight of passing trains. If this wasn't done, the leaf detritus would compromise traction and increase the likelihood of wheel slippage during braking. On 20 October 2022, in lovely late afternoon light, with autumnal colours evident on the trees, 66139 and 66011 pass Hungerford Common with 3J41, the 14.51 Didcot–Didcot RHTT working. Although based out of Didcot, 3J41 covers the Berks and Hants Line via Reading, running to Westbury and back, before returning to Didcot in the early evening.

Right: 66151, 66152 and their tanks spray their way round Crofton curve with 3J43, the Mondays only 02.52 Didcot–Didcot RHTT on 22 November 2021. I was hoping for a rainbow effect with the backlit spray, as Ivo Peters had filmed something similar back in the 1960s from a locomotive picking up water on Dillicar troughs, but the angle obviously wasn't what was needed to create this.

Above: Some years produce much more vivid autumnal colours than others. After a long, very dry and at times brutally hot summer in 2022, many trees turned colour earlier than usual and produced spectacular shows of yellow and gold. A very still, cool morning at Crofton has allowed mist to form just above the canal, with mirror like reflections from the trees, as the rising sun just catches their tops. 66041 and 66002 double head 6A53, the 05.13 Tytherington–Appleford on 6 October 2022.

Below: Less than an hour after sunrise and the track is still in shadow, but the surrounding countryside at Standers Foot Crossing is illuminated in stunning morning light that shows off the autumn colours. DC Rail's 60046 "William Wilberforce" takes its rake of spotless Cappagh-branded box wagons up the gradient towards Little Bedwyn, forming 6Z33, the 05.07 Willesden–Bristol FLT empties on 17 November 2021.

Left: The autumn colours in 2021 took much longer to develop. Some of the trees at Standers Foot Crossing on 1 November 2021 are still turning, while others have lost all their leaves entirely. 59205 drops downhill towards Hungerford at the head of 7A09, the 07.12 Merehead–Acton.

Below left: There was a fine autumnal display on the trees at Manningford Bruce on 22 November 2021, as 59004 "Paul A Hammond" slowly accelerates 7A09, the 07.12 Merehead–Acton, away from Woodborough Loops. 59004 had to make a standing start with over 4000 tonnes in tow. Even with the brief respite of the Pewsey dip, it will be more or less at full power for the nearly nine miles to Savernake Summit and the driver will not want to encounter any wheelslip caused by leaf fall.

Below: Sometimes the combination of sunlight, autumnal colours and the sky combine to produce a stunning scene. That was the case at Wolfhall on 9 November 2021, as 802014 passed with 1A77, the 08.35 Plymouth–Paddington. Unfortunately, the clouds then rolled in before any other trains appeared. Vegetation clearance on the approach to Savernake Summit in the background has resulted in some of the buildings of the former M&SWJR Savernake High Level station becoming partially visible.

Above: On 22 November 2020, 66509 heads 6Y15, the heavy 07.38 Tackley–Fairwater Yard high output ballast cleaner (HOBC) working. 66533 was on the rear of the train, beyond the bridge at Hungerford Common in the background. The wide trackbed here used to accommodate Hungerford Down Loop, but that was removed after the Newbury resignalling scheme was completed in 1978.

Above right: 66619 is about to pass under Oak Hill overbridge hauling 6A82, the 04.37 Whatley–Hayes and Harlington on 9 November 2021. Running at such an early hour, this is not normally a working that can be photographed at this time of year, but on this occasion it was running over three hours late.

Right: This final look at the autumnal colours of 2022 was captured well into the golden hour when the lighting was excellent. It highlights the orange livery of the locomotive and the surrounding foliage at Hungerford Common, as 59203 passes with a very short 7C77, the 12.15 Wembley–Merehead empties on 23 November 2022.

Chapter 10 – Crossings

Sometimes fortune conspires so that trains from either direction arrive at the photographer's location at the same time. This can be very lucky and result in an enhanced photograph, or very unlucky when the intended subject of the picture disappears behind another train, and the margin between the two outcomes can be very narrow indeed! This chapter portrays a selection of such photographs taken on the Berks and Hants Line over the years.

Above: This was a close shave at Beech Drive Crossing on the evening of 10 August 2021. 66515 was running 52 minutes late with 6X08, the 16.16 Fairwater Yard–Slough West HOBC working, tailed by 66561 as seen on the left. It had only just cleared the crossing as 66502 "Basford Hall Centenary 2001" approached just one minute behind schedule at the head of 6C62, the 16.50 Oxford Banbury Road–Whatley empties. Detail differences between the seemingly identical locomotives have crept in over the more than 20-year lifespan of the Class 66s. In this picture 66561 still has its original light clusters, whereas 66502 has been updated with more modern LED versions.

Below left: 23 August 2014 was a busy day on the Berks and Hants as the GWML was closed for engineering work at Reading. Services for Bristol and Cardiff were using the route as far as Westbury. On the right, HST power car 43140 "Landore Diesel Depot 1963 Celebrating 50 Years 2013/Depo Diesel Glandŵr 1963 Dathlu 50 Mlynedd 2013" leads an eastbound service past Great Bedwyn, while another HST passes Bedwyn station with a westbound train. Taken adjacent to the well-used Great Bedwyn Church foot crossing, I witnessed the world's luckiest dog, as it appeared on the canal side of the line, slipped through the gate, dodged these two HSTs as they crossed and came out unscathed through the gate on this side!

Right: Some crude patch painting has been undertaken by Freightliner on 59205 to remove the branding of its former owner DB Schenker. It is passing under the overbridge at Wolfhall working 7C64, the 15.25 Acton–Merehead empties on 14 July 2021. A GWR IET is heading in the opposite direction at reduced speed forming 1A89, the 15.38 Exeter St Davids–Paddington; this had crawled all the way from Pewsey, possibly because of the risk of rail buckling due to the high temperatures that day.

Above: Seconds after taking a photograph of 50001 "Dreadnought" powering up to Savernake Summit with 1A46, the 09.12 Penzance–Paddington on 14 June 1986, the view of the coaches was blocked by a Class 59/0 descending the bank with empties bound for Merehead Quarry. The Class 59 remains unidentified as it was yet to be named. The original four Yeoman 59/0s received their nameplates two weeks later on 28 June 1986 at Torr Works, Merehead.

Above left: On 17 March 2022 59002 "Alan J Day" has just passed over Sharcott Foot Crossing, Manningford Bruce at the head of 7A77, the 12.03 Merehead–Theale as a walker looks on, while 66606 comes around the corner with 7Z60, the 11.16 Brentford–Merehead empties. The foot crossing marks the start of the just under half a mile section of level track at the bottom of the Pewsey Dip, before the climb to Savernake Summit resumes.

Left: 59202 approaches Fairfield Foot Crossing near Little Bedwyn with 6L21, the 13.21 Whatley–Dagenham, while 59102 "Village of Chantry" heads away from the camera with a rake of JHA hoppers forming 6C74, the 14.55 Theale–Whatley empties on 27 June 2022. Foster Yeoman started using JHAs in 1989 after an unsuccessful experiment with a batch of aluminium bodied PHAs proved that these weren't strong enough to stand up to the demands of aggregate traffic. ARC followed with its own JHAs in 1990; this was obviously a good investment as the wagons are only starting to be withdrawn now, after more than three decades of hard work.

Above: The driver of the IET forming 1C92, the 18.03 Paddington–Penzance waves to his colleague on the IET forming 1K83, the 18.14 Bedwyn–Paddington, as it accelerates away from Hungerford and past the Common on 1 June 2019. At the time, IETs had just completed the full takeover from HSTs on long-distance services out of Paddington, so sights like this had started to be common; the turnback siding at Bedwyn had been lengthened to accommodate IETs. Post Pandemic however, off peak Bedwyn services have reverted to two or three-car Class 165 Turbo units.

Chapter 11 – Liveries

Very little remains the same for long on the railways and liveries are no exception. From the standard Rail Blue of the 1970s and early 1980s, through to the explosion of post-privatisation colour schemes and some one-off variations, the variety never ceases. This chapter examines some of the most common liveries to be seen on Berks and Hants Line over the last four decades. Not every livery that has been seen on the route is illustrated, as that would require an entire book!

Above: During the first half of the 1980s, summer Saturdays on the Berks and Hants were dominated by one of two locomotive liveries. Firstly, 47235 shows off the long-lived BR (or Monastral) Blue. The colour had been introduced in the mid-1960s and dominated for many years, until the liveries of the various rail sectors began to take over from the beginning of the 1980s. 47235 is seen bringing 3A27, the Plymouth–Paddington empty newspaper vans round Crofton Curve on 3 August 1985.

Abov right: This was the other livery that was seen every summer Saturday on the Berks and Hants Line during the early 1980s. Large Logo livery was introduced experimentally in 1978 on 56036 and on 47170 "County of Norfolk" in 1980. It was then applied to all new Class 56s from 56084 onwards and to Class 50s when they were refurbished. The first 50 to exit Doncaster Works carrying the new colour scheme was 50023 "Howe" in 1980. 50043 "Eagle" is also seen on Crofton Curve with 3A27 on 14 June 1986; it is one of a number of 50s that received black roofs rather than the standard grey.

Right: 1986 saw the introduction of Network SouthEast livery, with Class 50s being some of the first locomotives to receive it. Just over a month after the livery was introduced, 50023 "Howe" nears Bridge No. 99 with 3A27, the Plymouth–Paddington empty newspaper vans on 19 July 1986. Changes that had taken place a few months earlier were about to signify the end for newspaper trains. In January 1986, the News International Group had moved the printing of its papers to a new facility at Wapping in London. This utilised the latest technology, which meant that far fewer staff were required in newspaper production, triggering a year-long industrial dispute with the print workers' unions, as many of their members had lost their jobs with the move to Wapping. At the same time, the company moved distribution of its papers from rail to road, as it anticipated the rail unions opposing the changes it had made and preventing its members working newspaper trains carrying News International publications. The lengthy dispute ended in defeat for the unions and a domino effect ensued, whereby most other national newspapers also moved from Fleet Street to Wapping and changed to using road transport. Consequently, 150 years of newspaper distribution by rail came to an end in 1988.

Above: Railfreight Grey livery started to appear on the Berks and Hants Line later in the 1980s, mainly on Class 56s. 56039 is seen approaching Bridge No. 99 with a rake of empty POA four-wheeled box wagons on 22 June 1989. The POAs were built by Tiger Rail in 1988 using the chassis from redundant tank wagons to quickly provide additional rolling stock for the Mendip aggregates traffic that was supplying stone for the M40 construction project. These 46-tonne capacity wagons were often used on flows through Didcot and Oxford around this time.

Above right: From 1986 Foster Yeoman took a revolutionary approach to railway operations with the introduction of the first privately-owned locomotives to run on the national network. The new Class 59s were delivered in a clean, simple, silver livery with blue stripes at the top and bottom of their bodysides and Yeoman branding. Also noteworthy was the limited yellow on the cab ends, with only a half panel and even that was interrupted by the continuation of the lower bodyside blue stripe across the front. 59004 "Yeoman Challenger" brings a rake of empty four-wheeled hoppers past Wolfhall on 19 July 1986.

Right: In 1987, BR's Railfreight sector introduced a fresh corporate identity based around a new triple grey livery with bright and colourful sub sector emblems on its locomotives' bodysides. The Mendip aggregates traffic came under the auspices of Railfreight Construction and the unique 47901 displays the sub-sector's markings at Wolfhall with empties on 22 June 1989. Starting life as standard Class 47 D1628 and becoming 47046 under TOPS in November 1973, it was severely damaged in a derailment near Peterborough in 1974. It was repaired, but was then selected as the testbed for the engine chosen to power the projected Class 56s, so was fitted with a 16-cylinder Ruston Paxman 16RK3CT engine rated at 3250 hp and renumbered 47601. In 1979, once the Class 56 build programme was well underway, it was further converted to accommodate the engine earmarked for use in the future Class 58s. It was fitted with a 12-cylinder Ruston Paxman 12RK3ACT engine rated at 3300 hp and was renumbered 47901 to reflect its unique status, After that second period of testing was completed, 47901 spent the rest of its life working out of the Mendip quarries until withdrawal in March 1990. It was scrapped by MC Metals of Glasgow in February 1992.

Above: ARC-liveried 59101 "Village of Whatley" is seen from the north side of the line at Wolfhall, which is a view not often seen in print as the sun is only behind the photographer early in the day. It is hauling 6A18, the 05.45 Whatley–Southall on 12 April 1995. The four Class 59/1s entered service in November 1990, after they were built for Amey Roadstone Construction (ARC). They were delivered in this mustard yellow livery with grey roofs, cabs, bogies and underframes, and yellow half panels on the cab fronts. 59101 received a modified version of ARC livery around 1998; this consisted of mustard yellow with a thick silver stripe on the lower bodysides and front ends. *Terry Gurd*

Right: 59002 "Alan J Day" brings empty box wagons around Crofton Curve on 17 March 2009. The locomotive is in the revised Yeoman livery that was introduced in 1998. This still had a base colour of silver, but also included a broad light blue stripe along the side and across the cab windows. The amount of yellow on the cab front was further reduced to cover only the area between the light clusters and the buffers. This livery lasted on the class until around 2015.

Above: ARC was acquired by Hanson in 1988, after the 59/1s had been ordered, but before they were delivered in ARC livery. Hanson subsequently demerged a number of its constituent companies from 1996, but retained its construction businesses, including ARC under the Hanson name. In 1998 the Class 59/1's started to appear in this blue and grey Hanson livery, which includes an orange/red section on the roof and a yellow panel on the lower front end, and this colour scheme can still be seen today. On 17 March 2022, 59103 "Village of Mells" was photographed running downhill from Savernake Summit at Wolfhall with 6M20, the 10.38 Whatley–Churchyard Sidings.

Above: On 11 September 2020, 59205 and 59005 "Kenneth J Painter" pass Crofton Pumping Station hauling 7A09, the 07.12 Merehead–Acton. 59205 is wearing de-branded DB Schenker red, while 59005 is in the livery of Aggregate Industries, which had acquired Foster Yeoman in 2006. Aggregate Industries livery consists of a thin silver band that runs right round the locomotive, just below window level. Above this is mid blue, with turquoise below. The ends match the body colours, with yellow buffer beams. A large silver triangle is on the side, with a blue triangular logo at the top and the company's name in turquoise text below.

Above: 59204 wears the most recent livery to have been applied on the Class 59s, Genesee & Wyoming orange, with black stripes, a grey roof, Freightliner branding and a return to full yellow cab ends. So far, the colour scheme has only been applied to the ex-National Power/DB Schenker Class 59/2s, but as Freightliner now owns all the 59s except for 59003, it remains to be seen if this livery will be extended to the ex-Yeoman 59/0s and the Hanson 59/1s. The working is 6C31, the 10.08 Theale–Whatley empties, as seen at Great Bedwyn on 10 October 2022.

Above: HSTs have appeared on the Berks and Hants Line over the years in many different liveries, from the blue, grey and yellow of the original InterCity livery through to GWR's rather uninspiring green. 43002 and its Mark 3 coaches are in the penultimate of these liveries, First Great Western's purple with "Dynamic Lines". The train rounds Crofton Curve as 1C10, the diverted 10.27 Paddington–Bristol on 24 January 2015. As it was the first production power car to enter service in 1976, in May 2016 43002 was repainted into its original 1970s retro livery, which it carried during its last few years of service.

Above: In recent years, many special liveries have actually been vinyls stuck onto the recipient rather than paint. Such was the case for IET 802020, onto which GWR applied a Thank You livery for NHS workers during the Covid Pandemic in 2020. 802020 leads another unit at Manningford Bruce on 24 February 2022 forming 1C82, the 13.04 Paddington–Plymouth.

Above: Whilst DB Cargo-liveried Class 60s were an everyday sight on the Berks and Hants Line for many years working the inbound Robeston to Theale tanks, and from December 2019 to August 2022 on the return empties too, visits on other workings have been far rarer in recent years. For a few months before Freightliner took over the Mendip Rail contract in November 2019, DB Cargo 60s started to make appearances on the flow to and from Oxford Banbury Road. Here we see 60024 "Clitheroe Castle" working past Crofton Lock No. 60 with 6C58, the 11.45 Oxford Banbury Road–Whatley empties on 13 September 2019.

Above: 60066 was released into traffic after its Super 60 overhaul in December 2013, painted in a new silver livery with "Drax Powering Tomorrow" graphics in recognition of a trial run of Biomass traffic to Drax Power Station. It visited the Berks and Hants Line on 4 January 2020, when it was photographed hauling 6B33, the Saturday diverted 12.15 Theale–Robeston empty tanks, as seen on Crofton Curve.

Opposite page: From November 2019 DC Rail (DCR) took delivery of four Super 60-overhauled Class 60s which have seen use on the Berks and Hants Line mainly for short-term aggregate traffic flows. This resulted in two further Tug liveries appearing on the line. Firstly DCR's standard light grey, as displayed on 60046 "William Wilberforce" at Canal Bridge No. 99 with 6Z50, the 09.53 Willesden–Machen empties on 11 July 2022. The other DCR livery is the bright blue applied to 60028 with Cappagh branding (the parent company of DCR), which became a common sight on the Berks and Hants during spring and early summer in 2022, seemingly powering almost all of DCR's trains on the route at the time. 60028 brings 6Z50, the 09.44 Willesden–Machen empties towards Crofton Crossing on a perfect spring day, 26 April 2022. Regardless of their livery, Class 60s usually have their lamp clusters painted black, but in this case those on 60028 are yellow.

Above: This photograph allows us to contrast Class 66 liveries as 66150 and 66169 come round the curve at Kintbury hauling 6Z53, the 05.13 Tytherington–Appleford on 2 December 2021. 66169, which is still in its original yellow and red EWS livery, is looking scruffy after some 20 years in use, while 66150 wears DB Cargo red with "We are the future" branding to signify it being the first locomotive to be tested on the main line powered by hydrotreated vegetable oil.

Above right: In 2019 DB Cargo (DBC) signed an agreement with Maritime Transport for the latter to run DBC's freight terminals at Trafford Park in Manchester, Birch Coppice in Birmingham and Wakefield Europort. Several Class 66s have been repainted into this blue Maritime livery and named to mark the contract. 66051 "Maritime Intermodal Four" is in sole charge of 6M15, the 07.07 Tytherington–Calvert as it climbs past Wootton Rivers on 7 September 2021.

Right: 47580 "County of Essex" was in BR days a long-time resident of Stratford Depot in East London, spending ten years largely working on the Great Eastern main line until it was reallocated in 1988. In the 1980s, 47580 was given the trademark grey roof that many of Stratford's other engines received, but this modern variation of a Stratford livery was actually inspired by that carried by 47163 and 47164 during the 1977 celebrations for Queen Elizabeth II's Silver Jubilee. It includes the silver roof and large bodyside Union Flags, which were the first significant deviation from BR's standard blue livery. The flag seen on 47580 is the later and more accurate version, as those originally applied to 47163 and 47164 were decidedly poor reproductions that were quickly replaced. 47580 includes some visible embellishments and detail differences, including a plaque and Stratford depot's symbol from the 1980s, the Cockney Sparrow. In addition, neither 47163 or 47164 carried names in 1977. 47580 is bringing up the rear of 1Z60, the 08.34 Paddington–Salisbury "Cathedrals Express" railtour at Crofton on 28 May 2016, with 60103 "Flying Scotsman" on the front.

Chapter 12 – Then and Now

Railway photographic locations evolve over time. This can be due to the growth or removal of trees and vegetation, or it can be the result of changes to the railway or the surrounding infrastructure. In addition, different types of motive power come and go, with some only being seen on particular routes for short periods or during occasional visits. When images of a location that have been taken at different times are viewed side by side, sometimes striking differences are obvious, whereas some remain largely unchanged. This final chapter presents a selection of then and now views to illustrates some of the changes through time on the Berks and Hants route.

Above: 56049 wears the later variant of Railfreight Grey livery, complete with a red stripe, as it passes beneath the concrete footbridge at Little Bedwyn with a rake of empty four-wheeled hoppers on 22 June 1989. This view is relatively open, with the reverse curves back to the house by Fairfield Foot Crossing and the canal as far as Fore Bridge No. 92 both being visible.

Above: 66528 passes the same spot on 22 February 2022 with 6V18, the 11.20 Allington–Whatley empties. Over 30 years' worth of unrestricted vegetation growth beside the railway and canal has completely obscured the view down the track and Fore Bridge is barely visible. The conifer on the left has been allowed to grow for so long that it now encroaches over the eastbound track; note the indentation on its right, caused by passing trains which prevent it from spreading into the area that trains use.

Above: This view from the overbridge at Hungerford Common shows that summer Saturdays in the 1980s were not always blue skies and sunshine. 47240 rounds the curve shortly after a heavy shower hauling the 14.40 Paignton–Paddington on 24 August 1985.

Above: By 2015 the wide open vista from the 1980s has all but disappeared, with large mature trees populating the embankment on the left. Beyond the now-obscured canal on the right, a grove of Poplar trees has grown from nothing and this now blocks much of the remaining view. 59002 "Alan J Day" passes with 7A09, the 07.12 Merehead–Acton on 3 September 2015. In 2018 Network Rail cleared the cutting here of most of the trees and undergrowth, almost restoring the 1985 view, but no further maintenance has since been carried out and the view is once again disappearing behind greenery.

Above: On a wonderful summer's day by the Kennet and Avon Canal, as seen from the top of Bridge No. 99, 56043 rumbles past with a rake of empty hoppers that are bound for Merehead on 15 June 1985. Notice the width of the canal, the open view on the left and the low hedge on the right.

Above: Freightliner's pink ONE-liveried 66587 "As One, We Can" is seen from Bridge No. 99 on 28 November 2021 at the head of 6Y17, the 06.55 Didcot East Junction–Westbury engineering working. Reeds and undergrowth have reduced the width of the canal and the view of the adjoining fields has all but vanished behind new trees. Fortunately, the canal side of the railway has remained relatively free of vegetation and this remains a popular photographic spot today.

Right: 50031 "Hood" passes Fairwood Junction signal box on Saturday 27 August 1983 with 1A55, the 11.14 Paignton–Paddington. This isn't quite the classic 1970s scene, with lower quadrant semaphore signals and mature Elm trees on the right, but at least the box was still in use and the pointwork was manually controlled in 1983. This was however, the last summer before the Westbury resignalling project was commissioned. One of the new signals, which is not yet in use, can be seen in the distance beyond the train. The new layout and signalling was brought into use over the weekend of 11–14 May 1984, after which Fairwood Junction box was closed and demolished.

Above: On 14 July 2022, 66591 takes the road towards Westbury station at the head of a Class 6 VSTP (Very Short Term Planning) working, the 09.25 Whatley–Oxford Banbury Road. Even though the signal box has gone, considering that nearly 39 years has passed, the scene is remarkably similar. Unlike at many other junctions, the switched diamond crossing has been retained, although it appears to have been relaid and modernised with cast crossing Vs. The rail sides have been painted white to help combat rail expansion during hot weather; this simple practice allows the track to tolerate an additional five degrees Celsius. On this particular day there was a temporary speed restriction over the diamond and Network Rail staff were present to monitor the situation.

Above: Looking in the other direction at Fairwood Junction, the Westbury avoiding line can be seen swinging away to the right, with the two lines to the station on the left. Westbury's two main landmarks are visible in the background, the White Horse on Westbury Hill below Bratton Camp Hill Fort and the 400-foot chimney of Westbury Cement Works. 59103 "Village of Mells" heads west with 7Z85, the 12.45 Merehead–Exeter Riverside on 14 April 1997. *Terry Gurd*

Above: 66550 accelerates 6C68, the 11.38 Avonmouth–Whatley empties, away from a signal check and towards Fairwood Junction, while 59204 disappears into the distance with 7A77, the 12.03 Merehead–Theale on 14 July 2022. Like at most locations, the main difference here is the enormous amount of tree growth. The lack of vegetation management beside the avoiding line is breathtaking, with trains practically touching the trees. Another change, if the skyline on the left could be seen, is that the chimney of Westbury Cement Works has gone; the works was mothballed in 2009 and the chimney was demolished in September 2016.

Above: On 13 June 1987, 47436 is seen where Grafton East Junction used to be, with 1A34, the 09.30 Paignton–Paddington. The course of the former M&SWJR avoiding line used to run where the farm building is in the distance. At the time in 1987, work had just started on restoring Crofton Lock No. 57 which is beside the dry canal bed on the extreme left.

Above: 59206 "John F Yeoman Rail Pioneer" is slightly closer to the camera than 47436 is in the previous photograph. It is passing with 7A77, the 12.03 Merehead–Theale on 21 October 2021. The occupation bridge that used to cross the line here has been removed, but the same view is still available from the former approach embankment. The view of the canal and the area round the corner towards Wolfhall has vanished, although the farm building in the distance remains as a reference point. The site of the former junction is now used by Network Rail and is often covered in engineering detritus.

Above: Crofton Curve is one of the iconic Berks and Hants views, as seen from the overbridge that carries the road past Crofton pumping station. 50048 "Dauntless" swings round to the north-east at the head of 1A33, the 08.30 Paignton–Paddington on 3 August 1985. Although it is nowhere near as neat and tidy as it was in the steam era, the whole scene here is still quite open.

Above: 59001 "Yeoman Endeavour" brings a short 7A09, the loaded Merehead to Acton, around Crofton Curve on 13 June 2012. The more cluttered view here is rapidly disappearing behind the foreground bushes, while the occupation bridge beyond the train has vanished from sight. Fortunately the bridge's embankment was cleared after the bridge was removed some years later.

Above: The Friday before the May Day Bank Holiday weekend in 1986 produced the usual crop of additional locomotive-hauled workings to the West Country. Here we see 50048 "Dauntless" with the 15.47 Paddington–Plymouth relief service passing the former M&SWJR junction at Wolfhall on 2 May 1986. 25 years after the closure of the M&SWJR and the trackbed of the line on the right is still visible, as are the embankment and bridge abutments in the background.

Above: On 9 May 2015, the avoiding line embankment is barely visible anymore and accessing it would probably involve the use of a machete! Colas Rail's 60076 climbs past Wolfhall at the head of 6V62, the 11.12 Tilbury Riverside–Llanwern empty steel service, which had been diverted via the Berks and Hants Line because of engineering work that was taking place at Reading.

Above: On 7 September 1985, 50019 "Ramillies" brings 1A19, the 11.05 Penzance–Paddington under the occupation bridge that crosses Crofton Curve; the bridge was known to Network Rail as Lord Bruce's Bridge. In 1985 it was used by the local farmer to access the field inside the curve on the right. Even though its span was made from wrought iron and it had a severe weight restriction, it was regularly used by small tractors in the mid-1980s. By the 2010s though, it was obvious from the state of the access track that no motorised traffic had used the bridge in many years.

Above: Lord Bruce's occupation bridge was removed by Network Rail in 2016. Other than providing railway photographers with a vantage point, it no longer served any useful purpose, as the landowner could access the field on the right from near the pumping station. On 23 June 2020, 66952 is seen passing the now-redundant embankments, running light engine as 0Y08, the 09.45 Taunton–Reading.

Above: On 24 August 1985, 50026 "Indomitable" is just clearing the last stretch of the 1 in 132 incline to the former site of Savernake Low Level station with 1A33, the 10.50 Paignton–Paddington. To the right of the locomotive, a platform used to extend to where the two vehicle tracks appear to end, while the tracks themselves mark where the line into the bay platform used to be. The Down platform was on the left and ran to where the front of the locomotive is, with a water crane on the platform end ramp, then the junction signals and the pointwork for the Marlborough line beyond. The route of the former line to Marlborough can be seen curving away to the right. There was also a refuge siding towards the western portal of the canal tunnel, near the signal box which used to stand to the left of the grey hut in the background. The course of the M&SWJR's avoiding line to Marlborough is marked by the line of trees in the top right corner, while that of the GWR's branch is the next line of trees to the left. In its latter years, the signal box only opened on busy summer Saturdays. The station closed in 1966, and the box and the refuge siding survived until September 1978 when the Reading Panel Western Extension resignalling scheme was extended from Bedwyn to Woodborough.

Above: Some 38 years later and the views of the surrounding countryside have disappeared and the spreading undergrowth makes it difficult to imagine there was ever a station here. On 26 May 2023, 59005 "Kenneth J Painter" and 66568 bring 7A17, the 10.49 Merehead–Colnbrook up to Savernake Summit.

Above: On 26 August 1983, 47060 slowly brings a rake of empty former iron ore tippler wagons towards Frouds Lane overbridge, which is just west of Aldermaston. This type of wagon was amongst those first used by BR for aggregates traffic when Foster Yeoman moved transport of its products from Merehead Quarry from road to rail in 1970. By 1983 both Foster Yeoman and ARC had extensive fleets of their own privately-owned, modern, air-braked hoppers and box wagons, and use of these 1950s steam-era short-wheelbase wagons was coming to an end.

Above: 6 February 2023 was the date of my first visit to Frouds Lane overbridge since the previous photograph was taken in 1983. It's not just intrusive trees and undergrowth the rail photographer now has to deal with; the original view from the north side of the bridge is now hopelessly compromised by overhead line equipment and whilst the view here is broadly similar, that from the south has certainly not been enhanced by this modern addition. Over the nearly 40 years between these final two photographs, local passenger traffic to Newbury has progressed firstly from Class 117 DMUs to Class 165/166 Turbo units, and now to Class 387 EMUs, as 387145 illustrates with 2K44, the 13.12 Reading–Newbury.